MEN-AT-ARMS SERIES

EDITOR: MARTIN WINDROW

# Women at War
## 1939-45

*Text by* JACK CASSIN-SCOTT

*Colour plates by* ANGUS McBRIDE

OSPREY PUBLISHING LONDON

Published in 1980 by
Osprey Publishing Ltd
Member company of the George Philip Group
12–14 Long Acre, London WC2E 9LP
© Copyright 1980 Osprey Publishing Ltd

ISBN 0 85045 349 6

Filmset in Great Britain
Printed in Hong Kong

## Introduction

Images of warrior women come down to us from the most remote of ancient mythologies, invested with a significance as much religious as military. We read of Neith, the Libyan goddess of the Pelasgian religion, with her palace at Sais guarded by armed virgin priestesses who fought to the death each year for the honour of becoming high priestess. The Greek religion honoured Pallas Athene, embodiment of all the virtues of womanhood and none of the vices, goddess of storms and battle, wise in the ways of both peace and war. In Hellenic art Athene is always depicted in a warrior's helmet; when the United States WAACs of World War II adopted the helmeted head of the goddess as their Corps insignia, they were honouring a tradition many thousands of years old. Through the Hellenic myths come glimpses of the legendary Amazons, the proud race of women warriors reputed to rule a land to the south of the Black Sea.

In historical times the tale of the girl who cuts off her hair and 'goes for a soldier'—usually for the suitably romantic reason of following her soldier lover—is a recurrent theme. It crops up in the folklore of most of the world's armies, and is occasionally supported by documentary proof, as in the case of the famous Kit Davies of the Royal Scots Greys, who served as a dragoon in Marlborough's wars.

In the global wars of the 20th century women in uniform have become commonplace, for reasons of national necessity rather than personal adventure. So vast are the manpower needs of the modern state at war that in 1914–18 and 1939–45 hundreds of thousands of women, both volunteers and conscripts, served in an enormous range of capacities in the uniformed services, taking over any job which would free a man for combat duties. In Eastern Europe many thousands even crossed that ultimate barrier, and fought weapon in hand alongside their men.

The administrative and logistic needs of a sophisticated modern army are so vast, the proportion of rear-area manpower to fighting man-

British ATS lance-corporal in walking-out dress, wearing the basic khaki uniform with the red and blue forage cap of the Royal Artillery, and the RA badge pinned above the left breast pocket. See Plate A2. (Imperial War Museum)

ATS girl in full marching order, with gasmask satchel
strapped across the chest and gascape rolled and attached
to the shoulders. The water-bottle is slung on the left hip in a
leather 'cradle'; the steel helmet is looped by its chinstrap to
the left shoulder-strap of the tunic. The kitbag is dark blue.
(Imperial War Museum)

power so striking, that no state can afford to
ignore the potential contribution of women.
Against heavy initial opposition from conservative elements, women came to play a vital rôle in
the British war effort of 1914–18, though at this
stage almost exclusively on the home front. Their
social emancipation is generally recognized to
owe a direct and incalculable debt to their par-
ticipation. As in so many fields, the lessons of war
were forgotten in peacetime, and the outbreak of
World War II found the authorities unprepared
for the task of harnessing the willingness and skills
of the nation's women. Their contribution had
not been forgotten, however, and despite isolated
examples of resistance to the idea of women in the

services, the movement was not seriously hin-
dered. Once again hundreds of thousands of
women left the more or less narrow confines of
home life and learned to practise a multitude of
crafts and trades; and under the new conditions
of total war, the gap between their duties and
those of their menfolk grew ever narrower. Women
worked in munitions factories, on the railways and
the road transport systems, in a thousand different
clerical jobs, in sophisticated communications
duties, on combat airfields, at sea, in overseas
combat areas, as pilots, as searchlight crews on
operational anti-aircraft sites—their rôles became
integral with the national military effort, far
beyond their traditional province of nursing the
wounded.

Apart from the uniformed women's military
services of the main combatant powers, which
are the subject of this book, there were also many
volunteer organizations formed especially to aid
the civilian and military authorities. Their contribution, too, was incalculable, but to describe
them all would be impossible in a study many
times this size.

# Great Britain

### The ATS

The decision to raise the Auxiliary Territorial
Service for women as part of the Territorial Army
was taken on 9 September 1938; like all other
British women's services, this was a revival of the
concept which had short-sightedly been abandoned in the years after World War I. The grant
of a Royal Warrant gave women official status
as an integral part of the army, and by the outbreak of war on 3 September 1939 no less than
17,000 women had enlisted, under the leadership
of Dame Helen Gwynne-Vaughan.

The first units of the ATS joined the British
Expeditionary Force in France late in the winter
of 1939; these were bilingual telephonists who
manned army telephone exchanges in Paris.
Their short stay in France ended with the collapse
of the Allied armies in June 1940, and they were
evacuated, all arriving home safely on 16 June.
The next group to see overseas service were a
detachment of twenty officers who were trained

for technical intelligence duties at the Combined Services Detailed Interrogation Centre at Maadi, Cairo, arriving in December 1940. Security forbade the use of local labour, so they were supported by a group of cooks and orderlies, under the command of Company Commander Morrison Bell.

The two greatest demands on ATS womanpower came from the transport echelons, and Anti-Aircraft Command. By December 1940 AA Command was some 19,000 men short of establishment, and required 8,500 women immediately; but total female strength at that time was only 34,000, and recruitment—still voluntary —was almost at a standstill.

Neither industry nor the military were prepared for a long war, and manpower shortages became critical by mid-1941. It was estimated that the shortfall among both men and women would reach 300,000 by the middle of the following

*Left*
**ATS motor transport mechanics, wearing denim overalls of varying patterns over their battledress. Note cap details, including cloth chinstrap looped up over the crown. (Imperial War Museum)**

*Below*
**Queen Elizabeth (now H.M. The Queen Mother) inspecting with the late King George VI a parade of ATS personnel in winter dress. The greatcoats of officers and other ranks can be seen to be very similar; both could be closed to the throat if required. (Imperial War Museum)**

ATS subaltern—note 'pip' on greatcoat shoulder-strap—and lance-corporal on an Anti-Aircraft Command gun site, probably winter 1941. The helmeted girl wears her greatcoat over a battledress blouse and slacks. (Imperial War Museum)

In December 1943 the ATS Director, Chief Controller L. V. L. E. Whateley, C.B.E., stated that: 'In the United Kingdom there are more than 200,000 Auxiliaries and more than 6,000 officers. A third of these women are tradeswomen, qualified in a skilled trade to replace soldier craftsmen. There are 80 trades, fourteen of them Group 'A' trades calling for high qualifications, as armourers, draughtswomen, fitters, wireless operators.' These women were now entitled to wear on their uniforms the insignia of their trades. In addition there were fifteen different types of clerk among the 30,000 clerks; 9,000 technical storewomen; 3,000 teleprinter operators, and 4,000 switchboard operators.

The full range of duties performed by ATS personnel is too great to list. They supported or were attached to nearly all branches of the services, under army command; and in particular to the RE, RASC, RAOC and REME. Apart from the few trades mentioned above, they drove scores

year. A further 85,000 were required to increase the aircraft building programme. Consequently, on 2 December 1941, the War Cabinet announced the conscription of women, a step not systematically adopted by any other combatant power. The National Service Act made liable for compulsory service all unmarried women and childless widows. At first only those between the ages of 20 and 25 were called up; the limit was later dropped to nineteen, and could be extended to 30 if required. The Act made women eligible for all the traditional male decorations for service and valour, up to and including the Victoria Cross. Born of dire national need, this Act was to prove in the long run another huge step forward along the path of emancipation, and was a logical sequel to the previous Direction of Labour Act, 'conscripting' personnel into war industries.

By a Defence Regulation dated 25 April 1941 the ATS had been given equal status with men, coming under the Army Act, and their officers had been granted the King's commission—previously they had been appointed to their rank. (This status was also extended to medical personnel in the RAMC, to members of the WAAF, and to all those serving in the army and RAF nursing services.)

Traditional duties . . . an ATS sergeant cook, in white beret-style headgear and overall. (Imperial War Museum)

of different types of vehicles; they designed camouflage; they were involved throughout the departments concerned with photography, film-making and document micrograms, and in home-based intelligence agencies. They provided staff secretaries throughout the command echelons; worked in the plotting operations rooms of the Coastal Defences network; and helped satisfy the forces' insatiable hunger for maps in the various cartography establishments.

General Sir Frederick Pile, C-in-C Anti-Aircraft Command, was one of the first to suggest the use of the ATS on operational duties; regardless of some early opposition, the 93rd Mixed Searchlight Regiment was formed, and first saw action in mid-1942. (This was not the first use of women by AA Command, however; they had been present in various capacities on searchlight and gun sites before the end of 1940.) Although the training was mainly male-dominated, the field force consisted very largely of women officers and other ranks. Referring to their contribution, Gen. Pile said: 'The girls lived like men, fought their lights like men, and, alas, some of them died like men. Unarmed, they showed great personal bravery.' The use of ATS and Home Guard personnel released some 71,000 male gunners for other active service.

Demands for the services of the ATS came from all overseas theatres of war and Allied countries. Various units saw service in Canada, the USA, East Africa, India, and throughout the main war zones of the Middle East, Central Mediterranean, and North-West Europe. Training depots were set up in Palestine, Egypt, and Cyprus with local recruiting under ATS command, adding language problems to the normal frustrations of mobilization and training. Working alongside the ATS in these overseas areas were the Polish Auxiliary Territorial Service, with 502 Ambulance Car Company. The Polish women were particularly valuable during the build-up in Italy, performing clerical, hospital and general administrative duties apart from driving ambulances and other transport. Later ATS units were assigned to the teams of the Allied Commission which worked to take over the administration of the liberated territories until civil governments could be set up. On 28 July 1944 the advance

party of ATS personnel arrived at the rear headquarters of 21st Army Group in Normandy, and by December of that year had reached a strength of 6,290, including a strong element attached to SHAEF (Supreme Headquarters Allied Expeditionary Force).

\* \* \*

The Director and officers of the ATS were responsible for the well-being and moral welfare of the ATS personnel; and the public image of the service was an important factor, jealously guarded. This was not a problem shared by the nursing services, whose rôle had long been accepted in the public mind. It was the idea of 'women soldiers' which seemed to disturb some sections of the public; and malicious gossip and newspaper speculation about 'gross immorality' and bad living conditions were very prevalent at one stage. These allegations were investigated by a committee of enquiry under Miss Violet Markham, CH, which produced in August 1942 a very comprehensive report. The Markham Committee did offer some severe criticisms, and also sound recommendations for improvement in the

... and not so traditional. ATS girls are trained as firefighters, dressed in steel helmets, light khaki shirts and ties, and khaki slacks with wellington boots. The gasmask is slung ready for use, as always. (Imperial War Museum)

The ATS Band in its early stages; by May 1942 a corps of drums under a drum-major had been approved, and in April 1944 the band was recognized as a regular army band. (Imperial War Museum)

tually ran to eighteen printed pages! Special clothing was issued for special duties—overalls, wellington boots, leather jerkins, gloves, and of course the compulsory 'tin hat' when serving on AA sites. Khaki slacks and battledress blouses were worn on AA sites, with a three-quarter length fur coat with a deep collar being issued in cold weather.

Rank insignia were the same as for the male branches; but although ATS NCOs used standard army titles, officers had a special sequence of grades:

| | |
|---|---|
| Chief Controller | (Major-General) |
| Senior Controller | (Brigadier) |
| Controller | (Colonel) |
| Chief Commander | (Lieutenant-Colonel) |
| Senior Commander | (Major) |
| Junior Commander | (Captain) |
| Subaltern | (Lieutenant) |
| 2nd Subaltern | (2nd Lieutenant) |

**The WRNS**

The Women's Royal Naval Service, disbanded in 1919, was speedily re-established in 1939. The first recruits for the revived service were mainly drivers, writers, packers and domestic workers, with a few officers in command and some cypher officers in training. Over the war years more than 100,000 women were to see service in 90 rating categories and 50 officer categories, many calling for great technical skill; apart from administrative duties these occupations covered radar, radio and other specialized communications trades, and meteorology.

The numerical peak came in September 1944, with 74,620 women in uniform. In December 1945 the number had dropped to 48,866, and by June 1946 to a mere 15,000. Despite this rapid thinning out in the immediate aftermath of victory, the contribution of the WRNS was never in question. On 8 May 1945, VE Day, an Admiralty General Message to all stations at home and abroad, stated: 'The Board of Admiralty wish to record their highest appreciation of the part played by the Women's Royal Naval Service in support of the Fleet, and in the work of the Naval Command throughout the war against Germany and her European Allies. The loyalty, zeal and

field of living conditions; much of the bad management which had led to unsatisfactory conditions was soon rectified. In February 1942 a Directorate of Public Relations was formed to deal with ATS affairs, with PR officers in each army command. Special recruiting platoons and mobile exhibition platoons were set up to tour the country, and a band was formed as part of this public relations exercise, with a corps of drums under an ATS Drum-Major.

⋆    ⋆    ⋆

The first uniform issued was a khaki, belted army jacket with patch pockets, a khaki calf-length skirt, and khaki shirt, collar and tie. The headgear was a soft-topped khaki peaked cap with a cloth chinstrap and a 'turn-up' round the sides and rear of the band. This general style was to remain in use throughout the war. Later the ATS were allowed to purchase for 'walking out' wear the field service cap in the colours of the arm of service to which they were attached. Progressive modifications of the uniform generally followed the male patterns, and uniform regulations even-

efficiency with which the officers and ratings of the Women's Royal Naval Service have shared the burdens and upheld the traditions of the Naval Service through more than five and a half years of war have earned the gratitude of the Royal Navy.'

However, the WRNS were not given equivalent naval ranks to men, nor did they wear the distinguishing marks of naval officers; the justification, it is reported, was that they could not discharge the full duties of naval ranks and ratings. In this respect they were unique among the British women's services, and there was a long-running dispute over the fact that they were denied the full status granted to both the ATS and the WAAFs. The WRNS had their own code of regulations, and were not subject to the Naval Discipline Act, a provision which was described by Vice-Admiral Sir John Tyrwhitt, Bt., as 'a compliment to their womanhood'.

Many WRNS served on overseas stations, including the Middle and Far Eastern theatres of war. The first WRNS to serve afloat, on large troop-carrying transports, were Cypher Officers and Coder Ratings.

Basically the uniform worn by officers was an up-dated adaptation of that worn in World War I, influenced by current civilian modes of cut and style. The remodelled jacket allowed the top button to remain unfastened, a fact which Dame Vera Laughton Mathews, Director of the WRNS from 1939 to 1946, noted wryly when she recalled that she had been admonished for wearing a similar style in 1918. A pleated skirt came into use, shorter, tighter, smarter and much more decorative than the earlier pattern. The large tricorn hat of the old uniform was much reduced in size, becoming a jaunty-looking item rather more feminine in style than the officers' headgear of the other services; it was navy blue with black ribbon binding, and the RN officers' cap badge on the crown. It was later adopted by Chief Petty Officers and Petty Officers. The sleeve rank braid of the WRNS, as in World War I, was in a light blue shade; the 'curl' of male officers' ranking was replaced by a squared diamond shape. The usual width of the rank stripe was nine-sixteenths of an inch; the 'half stripe' was $\frac{1}{4}$in. wide, and the Director's sleeve was decorated with a $1\frac{3}{4}$in. stripe. Ranking was as follows:

| Superintendent | ... | Four stripes |
| Chief Officer | ... | Three stripes |
| First Officer | ... | Two and a half stripes, the 'half' between the thicker stripes |
| Second Officer | ... | Two stripes |
| Third Officer | ... | One stripe |

The uniform of ratings underwent a greater transformation. The jacket and skirt of navy blue became closer-fitting and more akin to civilian fashions. A white shirt-blouse and a black tie were normally worn under the jacket, and a dark blue shirt for 'fatigue' duties. For heavy duties a male style of clothing was issued: the white sailor's 'vest' with a squared neck edged in blue tape, and/or a dark blue, long-sleeved, round-collared jersey, with bell-bottomed sailors' trousers. WRNS despatch riders wore breeches and leggings, and either a soft peaked cap or a crash-helmet, with a duffle coat in winter.

In the early part of the war the authorities still favoured the Bond Street-inspired 'pudding basin' hat for ratings, a soft-crowned, wide-brimmed

Inspection of passes at the gate of a WRNS training establishment. The 'pudding basin' hats with the gold-lettered tally of HMS *Drake* date the photograph no later than early 1942. The CPO on the left is identified by her brass buttons and cuff buttons. The blue side-bags worn slung by the two ratings in the centre contain civilian-style gasmasks. (Imperial War Museum)

9

design which did not prove popular. Early in 1942 the male uniform 'sailor hat' was introduced, with some apprehension; but the new issue proved to be a great success throughout the service.

## The WAAF

Twenty-five years after the original WRAF had been disbanded, the nucleus which would become the new Women's Auxiliary Air Force was raised. The 1938 recruiting drive produced the personnel to form 48 Royal Air Force companies within the framework of the new Auxiliary Territorial Service.

These companies wore the ATS issue khaki uniform with RAF distinguishing insignia. The Chief Commandant of the ATS argued that the common use of the khaki uniform would not have a good effect on recruiting for the Air Force units, and suggested that a blue uniform 'would en-

courage loyalty, enthusiasm and good discipline'. By March 1939 the new uniform of RAF blue was authorized, although stocks of material were not immediately available.

The 48 companies were transferred as the nucleus of the new WAAF. The 'Aircraftwomen' paraded in a variety of strange guises in these early months, including a mixture of issued uniform items and civilian clothes. Official sources state that 'recruits were compensated for wear and tear of their civilian garments', and by December 1939 the accounts department had set up an allowance rate: two shillings per week for lack of a full uniform, ninepence for lack of a raincoat. The shortage of clothing became so acute that the whole recruiting drive had to be curtailed, and finally stopped. By early 1940, however, the Government was able to supply all members of the service with at least one complete uniform, although several more months would pass before they could equip them fully. Greatcoats for the winter of 1940, and further shirts and shoes, were the subject of continued supply pressures.

**The post-1942 WRNS uniform clearly displayed by a Second Officer (*left*), two Third Officers and two ratings. The ratings wear the 'sailor hat', without its white summer cover, and with the simple cap tally 'HMS', normal in wartime. (Imperial War Museum)**

*Above*
**A small WRNS working party about to swab decks, pre-1942. They wear the early model hat, also with HMS *Drake* cap tally; crew-necked dark blue sweaters; and rolled-up dark blue slacks. (Imperial War Museum)**
*Left*
**WRNS mechanics working on an anti-aircraft gun aboard ship. The 'dirty work' uniform consisted of a dark blue denim-type jacket and slacks, dark blue shirt and tie, and sailor hat. (Imperial War Museum)**

In April 1941 the first breakthrough in uniform practice came with the issue of a working battle-dress uniform to replace the long, belted, four-pocket jacket and skirt of the normal service dress. Specially designed for the use of WAAF balloon operators serving with the balloon barrage, this blouse and trousers were extremely popular, and there was an immediate response from all the other WAAF 'trades', each presenting a vigorous case for entitlement to the working uniform.

Once the teething troubles over uniforming the new service had been overcome, recruiting resumed, and continued at an ever-increasing rate. From a nucleus of just 2,000 members, with one officer class and six trades, strength had risen by late 1943 to 182,000, serving in 22 officer branches and 75 trades at home and abroad. By early 1943 the WAAFs represented 16 per cent of the RAF's total strength, and 22 per cent of the strength on the airfields under Home Command. By the end of the war 95 per cent of the women in uniform were replacing men in jobs which would otherwise have had to be filled by able-bodied airmen, and 70 per cent of them served in skilled trades. All technical and non-technical training courses established by the RAF were open to WAAFs; among the many trades they filled were those of riggers, fitters, welders, telephonists, storekeepers, operations room plotters, mapping

clerks, radar location personnel, drivers and orderlies. They served throughout the world, on nearly every RAF station at home and overseas, working alongside RAF male personnel in all their branches and trades. Their casualty rate was much higher, especially in the early part of the war, than that of other women's services. Those who ran the operations rooms at RAF fighter stations, and manned the coastal radar stations, were in the front line during the Battle of Britain in summer 1940, when the Luftwaffe carried out a prolonged, vigorous, and extremely effective campaign of direct bombing and strafing attacks on these establishments. The conduct of these WAAFs under fire showed that apart from being able to sustain their efficiency in boring and repetitive administrative jobs, women in uniform were perfectly capable of facing the danger of death and mutilation with as much steadfastness as their male comrades.

Unlike the other women's services, the WAAF became more and more closely integrated with the other branches of the RAF as its recruitment increased. They served under direct RAF command and, wherever possible, under the same regulations and discipline. This uniformity was underlined by the greater similarity of dress between male and female personnel. The cut of the jacket, skirt and cap followed those of the ATS,

**WRNS despatch rider in winter duffle-coat; see Plate C1. (Imperial War Museum)**

but with the same insignia as male personnel, apart from the cypher in the other ranks' brass cap badge. The other ranks' cap had a glossy black leather peak, and that of officers a cloth-covered peak. Officers wore the RAF officers' cap badge.

Officers' ranks in the WAAF changed in 1942, as follows:

| WAAF 1st pattern | WAAF 2nd pattern | RAF equivalent |
| --- | --- | --- |
| Senior Controller | Air Commandant | Air Commodore |
| Controller | Group Officer | Group Captain |
| Chief Commandant | Wing Officer | Wing Commander |
| Senior Commandant | Squadron Officer | Squadron Leader |
| Company Commander | Flight Officer | Flight Lieutenant |
| Deputy Company Commander | Section Officer | Flying Officer |
| Company Assistant | Assistant Section Officer | Pilot Officer |

Initially the NCO and other ranks' titles were Senior Section Leader, Assistant Section Leader, and Aircraftwoman 1st and 2nd Class. Later the rank of Under Officer was introduced, equivalent to the RAF's Warrant Officer, and the lower ranks were changed to the RAF equivalent— Flight Sergeant, Sergeant, and Corporal. Rank insignia was as for male personnel: pale blue on dark blue sleeve rings for officers, and pale blue on dark blue chevrons for NCOs.

## The ATA

The women of the WAAF did not fly operationally; Soviet Russia is believed to have been the only nation which had formal units of female combat troops. The British women pilots came from the pre-war Civil Air Guard, re-formed in 1939 under Gerard d'Erlanger as the Air Transport Auxiliary. In September of that year it had a mixed-sex membership of 22 pilots.

Like their American WASP counterparts, the ATA functioned as a ferry service, to deliver completed aircraft from the manufacturers to the airfields of the RAF. By the early part of 1940 the women pilots numbered 26, among them the famous pioneer airwoman Amy Johnson, C.B.E., the first woman to fly solo from England to Australia, and holder of a record for a flight to India. Amy Johnson died on 6 January 1941 when the Oxford aircraft she was ferrying crashed in the Thames Estuary.

By September 1941 the ATA pilots were flying all types of operational aircraft. By the end of the war they would have delivered 308,567 aircraft of more than 200 types, including Spitfires, Hurricanes, Mosquitoes, Blenheims, and the heavy four-engined Lancaster and Flying Fortress bombers. The strength of the ATA was 1,152 men, and 600 women including 166 pilots and four flight engineers. The women pilots performed exactly the same duties as the men, and had equal pay and rights from late 1943. Twelve women pilots, one woman flight engineer and a nursing sister were killed in the course of their duty.

The ATA uniform comprised a dark navy blue service tunic with four patch pockets, flapped and buttoned, and a cloth belt with a brass buckle. The plastic buttons had a raised crown and ATA cypher insignia. A shirt of WAAF blue was worn with a black tie. A blue skirt and slacks were provided, as respectively 'walking out' and air-

Women radio mechanics, who flew in Royal Navy aircraft during trials of equipment, dressed here in full flying suits and parachute harness for a flight in a Walrus ASR flying boat. (Imperial War Museum)

In 1927, however, there appeared in the Army List a reference to FANY, 'officially recognized by the Army Council as a voluntary reserve transport unit'. In 1937 the title became 'Women's Transport Service FANY'. The references to both nursing and yeomanry were now completely outdated, as driving was now the corps' main function. They were also fully trained in signals procedures and techniques, radio communications and map-reading. With the revival of the women's services in 1938 an ATS/FANY driving section was created, bringing into the young ATS an immediate transfusion of some 1,000 trained drivers. The War Office gave an assurance that the identity of the FANY would be fully preserved, and the 6,000 or so FANYs who served with the ATS wore their own scarlet shoulder flashes with the initials of their organization. Their main duty was training ATS drivers at their Camberley driving school. Under the National Service Act they became full members of the ATS. Their responsibilities later expanded in many areas, and as a voluntary organization they retained and financed their own London headquarters, training volunteer FANYs in many duties. They wore their own uniform, similar to that of the ATS but

field and flying wear. (Shirt, tie, and black shoes and stockings had to be privately bought.) There were also a dark blue greatcoat, and a Field Service cap of the same shade, with a brass badge on the left side at the front. Rank was indicated on the shoulder-straps, one and two gold stripes identifying Second and First Officers. A pair of gold embroidered wings were worn on the left breast by all pilots. The various developments of normal RAF flying clothing and boots were issued progressively, including Irvin suits.

## The FANY

Britain's first officially recognized uniformed women's service of the armed forces was born in 1907 with the formation of the First Aid Nursing Yeomanry—FANY. For various reasons, mainly attributable to lack of vision in official circles, the British army was denied much of their services in World War I; but many members served overseas with the Belgian and French armies, often exposed to enemy fire, and winning many awards for bravery.

Ratings acting as Royal Marines auxiliaries, wearing the dark blue uniform with a peakless dark blue cap enlivened by the Marines' gilt globe and laurel cap badge on a red cloth patch. (Imperial War Museum)

generally smarter and better fitting, with a Sam Browne belt. More than 8,000 FANYs served in a total of 22 countries during and after the war.

It was under cover of the FANY organization that a supremely gallant band of British and foreign women were trained for intelligence work with the resistance groups of occupied Europe. Smuggled behind enemy lines, usually by a night parachute drop, they played an extremely important rôle in the hideously dangerous activities of the liaison groups and the various underground cells. Casualties were high; some of these heroines have become household names, but many others who went to torture in Gestapo cellars and death in the concentration camps have remained anonymous. Their part in the operations of SOE was indispensable, their courage was beyond praise, and their achievements were extraordinary. To single out only one to represent this remarkable group of women, there was Captain Nancy Wake, who was

*Above*
**Parade of WAAFs under inspection by the late Duchess of Gloucester, showing the differences between the uniforms of other ranks and an officer of air rank. (Imperial War Museum)**

**Another WAAF inspection, this time by Queen Elizabeth, again showing a good contrast in the foreground between officers' and other ranks' uniform. (Imperial War Museum)**

**WAAF and RAF officers wearing greatcoats; the similarities between male and female uniform, which underlined the integration of the two services, are apparent here. (Imperial War Museum)**

parachuted into France in February 1944. Through the loss of several other leaders she became the commander of no less than 7,000 Maquis fighters in the Auvergne, rallying them and leading them in battle against the Germans when the time came to link up with the Allied armies which landed in the south of France.

# United States of America

There was an unfortunate lack of zeal and uniformity in the compiling of information on the early days of the American women's services in World War II, which handicaps the historian. Through lack of manpower, time or opportunity, or in some cases through a doctrinaire unwillingness to collect separate statistics for women, the various army departments failed to collate information in a systematic way. This omission does less than justice to the Women's Auxiliary Corps, which rose to a peak strength of some 100,000 members; and is the more obvious today, with

women moving further towards complete integration in the new volunteer US Army than their parents' generation would ever have thought possible.

It may generally be stated, however, that in terms of human and administrative problems, often unanticipated or inadequately thought through by the authorities, American experience closely followed that of Britain. America is and was no less conservative a society than Britain in its view of a woman's place in life. There was psychological resistance to the concept of women in uniform; and when the principle had been accepted, the special requirements in the fields of discipline, regulation of conduct and recreation, medicine and welfare, and the general problems of introducing girls to an army life and atmosphere, were often handled by trial and error. It was some time before the difficult problem of reconciling the needs to treat women equally with men, but not identically, was resolved. At what may be considered a rather trivial level, there was much argument over uniform design. The women had to be provided with a uniform military in appearance, with a maximum of comfort, style and fit, and yet not identical to that of the men. At a more serious level, which would centrally effect the success of the recruiting effort, the US Army had to stand as guarantor to the concerned public for a high standard of conduct, well-being and training for the women entrants. By the end of the war most, if not all, of these problems had been overcome. The boost given to the general cause of female emancipation by the women's services was enormous.

### The WAAC and WAC

It is interesting to note the haste with which plans for the formation of the women's corps were prepared following the attack on Pearl Harbor on 7 December 1941. The Secretary of War sent his approval of the WAAC Bill to Congress on 24 December. By the last day of that month a Mrs Rodgers had incorporated the War Department's proposed amendment into the Bill and reintroduced it as H.R.6293.

The Navy Department lacked confidence in the Bill and attempted to delay it, and to persuade the War Department to drop their sponsorship of the

Corps. They were induced to drop their objection, but decided to take no part in the venture. The Army Air Corps, however, put forward a very convincing argument in favour of the plan. They stated that if the WAAC Bill was not ratified, manpower shortages could put the east coast, and Washington itself, in actual danger. The Aircraft Warning Service could not be operated successfully with civilian volunteers, and only the formation of the Women's Auxiliary Army Corps would permit the maintenance of 'twenty-four-hour daily security'.

The 37-year-old wife of a former governor of Texas, Mrs Oveta Culp Hobby, was appointed into the position of WAAC Director. Her first task was a detailed study of the already well-established British and Canadian women's services. The pattern of public unease over alleged 'immorality', which had forced a strong official reaction from the British authorities in both World Wars, was repeated in the United States, and had to be dealt with by a concerted public relations campaign.

More practical problems also followed a very similar pattern on both sides of the Atlantic, and Mrs Hobby benefited from being able to study British experience, which was two years or more ahead in every field. In British experience there had been considerable reaction from the public and the military to the less than satisfactory efficiency and co-ordination of civilian voluntary organizations. Both the ATS and WAAF had been admitted to full military status. The women's division of the Royal Canadian Air Force was in effect an integral part of the RCAF, and had fewer administrative problems than the Can-

American WAAC recruits 'stand by their beds' for inspection. In the centre is WAAC Director Oveta Culp Hobby, in képi-style cap and light khaki summer uniform, the outcome of much discussion and the ideas of several different designers. (*Life*)

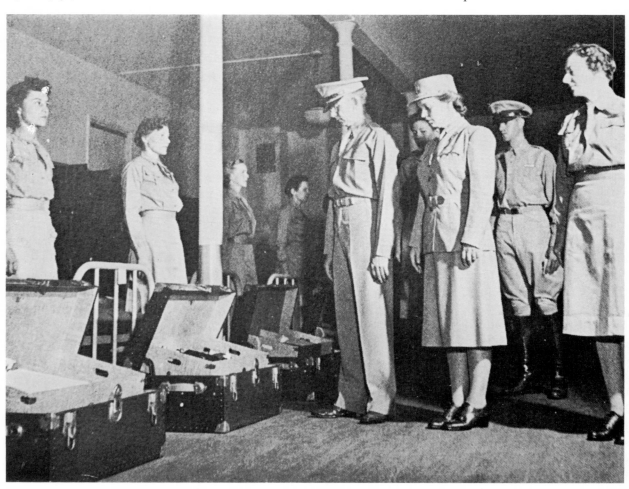

adian Women's Auxiliary Corps, which acted merely as an auxiliary force 'with' but not 'within' the army. The British and Canadian commands strongly disliked any element of separation in command structure, regulations or status for any members of their forces, and within a few months the Canadian WAC was to follow the example of the RCAF. It is also interesting that the WRCNS, at this period undergoing its initial organization, never made any attempt to operate without full naval status.

Another fruitful field of study for Mrs Hobby was the record of difficulty suffered by the Allies during rapid mobilization. Shortages of housing, uniforms, proper medical facilities, and—above all—shortages of really well-trained and experienced women officers all had to be faced by the ATS and WAAF in the early part of the war, and were overcome with considerable success by 1942, by which time the importance of the women's contribution to the war effort was widely accepted within and outside the military.

The saga of the WAAC uniform is worth recounting in some detail, as an example of the kind of practical problems faced by Mrs Hobby. The initial strength of the Corps was some 12,000, and clothing this number appeared to be within the capability of the Quartermaster General, whose department 'anticipated no unusual difficulties'. This proved to be one of the most chronic miscalculations of that worthy body.

The Standardization Branch assumed responsibility for the WAAC uniforms under the guidance of a Col. Letcher O. Grice. Because of the distinctive nature of the uniform, requested in the legislative authorization, the colonel procured sketches from famous dress designers of the day. The designers suggested a uniform in two shades of blue. Grice went further: he agreed that the uniform should be different not only in design but also in colour, and welcomed the idea of the two blues; these blues must not, however, bear any similarity to the blues currently worn by the Army Nurse Corps. The Standardization Branch was informed by the designers that the blue dyestuffs were available, and the alternative suggestion of a grey uniform was rejected on the grounds that grey was a difficult colour for matching.

The first discord to spoil this harmony was heard from the direction of Philadelphia. The Philadelphia Depot had not been informed of all the forward planning. Since research and development was the Depot's domain, they were not unnaturally annoyed that three months of discussions had progressed without their being invited to the party. Whether from pique or otherwise, their representative, who had no special knowledge of women's clothing requirements, declared that there should be 'nothing fancier for WAACs than for combat soldiers'. Director Hobby, who hoped that the WAACs would eventually become a part of the US Army proper, added her weight to this argument, along the lines that the uniform should be as close as possible to that of the soldiers.

The blue-vs.-Olive Drab argument dragged on, until common sense prevailed and the Philadelphia Depot won the point. Since stocks of Olive Drab and khaki (in British terms, 'khaki drill') had already been acquired, further purchases of blue material would have been wastefully expensive. Stock materials of covert and barathea for winter, and 8.2 khaki for summer were decided —although the latter subsequently proved too heavy for women's clothing.

The demand for a stylishly designed uniform was still on the table, so ideas were canvassed from famous designers such as Helen Cookman, Maria Krum, Mangone, Russell Patterson and Mary Sampson. A compromise was reached which perfectly exemplifies the way bureaucracies handle questions of taste. One or more of the salient features was taken from each of the designs, and a 'composite' was constructed from the bits! A collar came from one, a lapel from another, a pocket design from a third. Mangone had suggested that a belt would aid the appearance of the female figure. No, said the Quartermaster General, it would rub against the jacket and wear holes. A leather belt would be more attractive, said Maria Krum. Definitely not, said the QMG: if anything, the belt should be of cotton, which would be cheaper and would cause less friction. A pleated skirt was requested, but rejected in favour of a narrow six-gore skirt by the War Production Board, in line with restrictions on the use of material. Slacks were designed as part of the original uniform, but were discarded early on as too difficult to fit comfortably and inexpensively to a wide range of female shapes. The second choice of split-skirt culottes was rejected as being impractical for women working as mechanics. (At this time it was envisaged that motor transport would be the only outside work women would undertake, so it was believed that an issue of overalls would be sufficient and separate trousers would be unnecessary.)

After a good deal of thought it was decided that public reaction to over-masculine uniforms would be unfavourable, so skirts rather than trousers were specified. An open-neck blouse was rejected in favour of a more military and dignified khaki shirt and tie, in accordance with the Director's wish for as military an appearance as possible. Controversy over the headgear was intense, however, and lasted for most of the war.

For WAAC officers the QMG suggested a stiff service cap similar to that of the men, with the popular 'overseas cap'—or sidecap—for other ranks, and a khaki, brimmed hat for summer wear. The Director requested that officers and enlisted ranks should have the same hat, as being more democratic. Mrs Hobby considered that the widespread use of the 'overseas' type of cap by other voluntary organizations made it undesirable; there were solid reasons why the WAACs should be immediately distinctive. By a large vote a peaked cap was selected, as being practical in all weathers and military in appearance; it was of a 'peaked pillbox' or képi shape, in OD cloth.

A heavy top-coat designed by Mangone, very similar to that of the soldiers, was included in the issued uniform. A utility coat designed by Maria Krum replaced the field jacket of male personnel; it was in a lightweight material, with a raincoat styling, and had an attached hood and a button-in lining.

Since the issued uniform had no trousers, the only pockets were in the jacket. The carrying of personal items in the breast pockets produced some embarrassment, and orders were quickly given that not even a pack of cigarettes was to be carried. A shoulder-strap handbag was quickly issued to fill the gap. Brown Oxford-type shoes were worn for all normal duties, with plimsolls, galoshes and bedroom slippers for appropriate times. Rayon stockings were worn for 'walking out' and cotton ones for working dress.

The selection of an insignia for the WAACs was solved with a suggestion from the Heraldic Section of the QMG's office that the head of Pallas Athene be adopted. This wholly fitting suggestion was approved, and the helmeted female profile was worn in the usual manner—in 'cut-out' form by officers on both lower lapels, and on a brass disc on the left lapel by enlisted ranks, balanced by a disc with the national cypher. The cap badge was a plainer version of the American eagle than that worn by male branches, and was popularly known as the 'buzzard'. As the WAACs were an auxiliary corps they could not wear army buttons, so the 'buzzard' was embossed on their plastic buttons. Insignia of rank and grade generally followed army practice, with the letters 'WAAC' on a flash under the chevrons.

Predictably, these initial designs were found to be unsatisfactory in various ways as experience of their use accumulated, and new uniform patterns began to emerge in 1943 and 1944. The idea of their production was purely academic, however, as the large initial stocks acquired had to be used up before any new expenditure could be undertaken. The original peaked cap came in for criticism, and Director Hobby herself reversed her earlier decision and requested a change to the overseas cap in January 1943. This request was at first resisted, but was eventually granted. An issue of overalls to all personnel was granted to members of the women's services when, as a result of a rapid expansion in numbers and in duties undertaken, it became clear that many were doing jobs for which the 'walking out' and issued cotton fatigue dresses were equally inappropriate.

Women were now employed in many fields previously the exclusive province of male personnel. Aside from work in hospital wards and laboratories they were driving light trucks and staff cars, serving as messengers, welders, and full-time mechanics, and—in the Army Air Corps—working on the general maintenance of airframes and engines.

On 28 June 1943 (signed 1 July 1943) came the final decision to integrate the WAAC with the US

Army. The Congress passed a Bill requiring all personnel to choose between an honourable discharge or enlistment into the new Women's Army Corps, Army of the United States, as from 30 September 1943. On 5 July 1943 Director Oveta Culp Hobby became Colonel Hobby of the US Army, the first woman to be admitted to the new concept of the army. Her dream had come true, and the women's service would henceforward—like those of Britain and Canada—be 'in', and not just 'with' the Army.

## The Naval and Marine Services

There was strong resistance to the idea of accepting women into the ranks of the US Navy, but the service nevertheless acknowledged the existence of the WAVES (Women Appointed for Volunteer Emergency Service). Known equally as the Women's Naval Reserve Corps, they performed some of the same duties as the British WRNS —mainly administrative, but also domestic, secretarial and clerical, and in the communications branches. They held similar ranks to their male counterparts up to Lieutenant-Commander, drew the same pay, and served (as did the WACs and Women Marines) for the duration of the war plus six months. Their primary purpose was to relieve men for service at sea. They themselves served on shore duty within the continental limits of the USA, but not on combat vessels or aircraft.

The Navy avoided the worst of the clothing difficulties suffered by the Army by the simple expedient of granting WAVES a clothing allowance to purchase their own uniforms. Various commercial firms were authorized to manufacture uniforms to the official specification, and they were then sold through large department stores, which gave expert fittings. Shoes and other personal articles were chosen from standard commercial models available, and therefore the fit was generally better and more individualistic. In the long term the WACs benefited from the free replacement of worn-out articles, as the WAVES allowance of $12.50 paid quarterly was said to be insufficient to keep them in stockings, let alone all the other items.

Curiously the WAVES, with their stylish uniform designed by Main-Bocher, recruited far less women than either the WAACs or the WACs. Recruitment into the WAVES, SPARS (Coast Guard women's reserve, from the motto 'Semper Paratus') and the Marine Corps Women's Reserve varied constantly in close proportion to that of the WAACs. There was clearly more to the choice than a comparison of uniforms; possibly the limitation to service inside the United States, which applied equally to WAVES, SPARS and Women Marines, was a factor.

The MCWR was the US Marine Corps parallel to the Navy's WAVES. Regulations and conditions of service were closely similar to those of the male branch; pay was the same as that of the WAC. The highest rank was that of Major. Rank insignia was the same as for male officers and men. The uniforms varied with the season, as in the other women's services. Women marines carried out a wide range of duties, serving as stenographers, draughtswomen, orderlies and domestic workers, electricians, radio and film operators, parachute packers, etc.

On 31 May 1941 a revised edition of the US Navy Uniform Regulations was approved by the Secretary of the Navy. Chief among the many changes incorporated from earlier editions, from

**WAACs clean their billets. The jacket and képi can be seen more clearly here; note the name tag above the left breast pocket, worn by all recruits. (Life)**

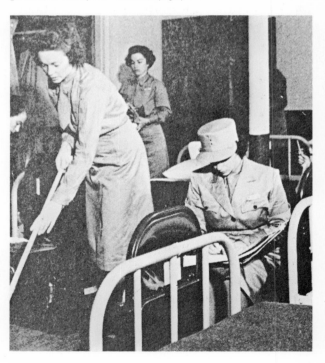

the point of view of women's services, was the inclusion for the first time of notes on the dress of the Navy Nurse Corps. Since its inception as early as 1908 the NNC had been dressed according to the instructions of the Chief of the Bureau of Medicine and Surgery, subject to the approval of the Secretary of the Navy.

Initially the Nurse Corps were not dressed in a military uniform, but in the ward dress of their civilian counterparts, a white duty costume, and a cap. Off duty they wore civilian clothes. In the May 1941 regulations only the ward uniform and outer protective clothing were specified, with the minimum indication of their attachment to the Navy. Shortly after the USA entered the war, it became clear that some form of outdoor military costume was necessary. An instruction of 20 March 1942 from the Chief of the Bureau of

Medicine and Surgery led to the Bureau of Navigation authorizing new uniform items for the Nurse Corps: blue and white service uniforms with blue and white caps, and a blue overcoat. A further instruction of 1 December 1942 described the uniforms in detail.

The white ward uniform, cap, raincoat and cape of the 1941 regulations remained unchanged. The new blue, winter service uniform had a double-breasted reefer jacket with two rows of three gilt buttons, buttoning on the left; a blue skirt and a blue cap. The jacket was worn over a white shirt and black tie. On the collar of the jacket were worn the branch devices of the NNC, the same on each side: a gold foul anchor with a gold oakleaf and acorn superimposed across the centre, the leaf bearing the cypher 'NNC'. Ranking was worn in the form of cuff lace, a sequence of gold or yellow stripes of $\frac{1}{2}$in. width, the 'half stripe' measuring $\frac{1}{4}$in. wide.

The white uniform jacket was single-breasted, with four pockets, three gilt buttons, and the

**WAAC recruits line up for 'chow'; issued the same ration as male GIs, they later had the calorie content reduced on the grounds that they burned up less energy than men. The light seersucker working dress had a cloth belt tied at the front; the 'pudding basin' hat was popular. (US Army)**

same 'rolling' collar and notched lapels as the blue outfit. In this dress the collar devices were worn on the shirt, and the ranking on stiff dark blue shoulder-boards in the form of conventional transverse stripes across the ends. The collar insignia also varied in that a rank device was worn on the right-hand shirt collar point, and the NNC insignia on the left point only.

Ranking paralleled US Navy commissioned ranks from lieutenant-commander down:

| Insignia on shirt collar (whites) | Insignia on shoulder-board (whites) and cuff (blues) | NNC Ranks | USN Ranks |
|---|---|---|---|
| Gold oak leaf | Two ½in. stripes, one ¼in. stripe between | Superintendent | Lt.-Cdr. |
| Two silver bars | Two ½in. stripes | Assistant Superintendent | Lt. |
| One silver bar | One ½in. stripe below one ¼in. stripe | Chief Nurse | Lt. (j.g.) |
| One gold bar | One ½in. stripe | Nurse | Ensign |

The caps had either blue or white crowns but were otherwise identical for both uniforms. In shape they resembled a male officer's peaked cap with the peak removed. The circular crown was about half an inch higher at the front than the back, and the black mohair band increased in width from ¾in. at the back to 1¼in. at the front. There was a half-inch gold lace chinstrap, with keeps and buttons, placed at the *top*, rather than the bottom edge of the band at the front; and the gilt NNC insignia was pinned to the front of the crown.

All in all, the December 1942 orders brought the appearance of the NNC uniform much closer to that of the US Navy proper.

A July 1942 modification of the 1938 Reserve Act allowed the enrolment of women in the Naval Reserve, creating new uniform problems for the Navy Department. On 20 March 1943 the Bureau of Naval Personnel issued uniform regulations for the Women's Reserve, but this document made no mention of current 1941 regulations. Given the Navy's attitude that the employment of women in uniform by the Navy was purely a temporary measure, it is not surprising that until 1948 WAVE uniform instructions were published separately from those of the rest of the service.

The Navy suffered from lack of experience of women's uniforms. The only authorized women's uniform in World War I was that of the 1917 'Yeomanettes', very far removed from military or civilian fashion of the 1940s. Following the Army example, the USN called on the expertise of such civilian designers as Main-Bocher. The final result was a very stylish, smart assemblage of military and civilian fashions, based on a blue or white single-breasted jacket with matching skirt, and a hat with a blue or white cover, for both officers and enlisted ranks.

In the women's services a democratic uniformity of dress for all ranks was always more noticeable than in the male services. In the WAVES the enlisted ranks wore the same jacket as officers but with blue plastic buttons. Officers and chief petty officers wore the same type of hat, with a stiffened oval crown and a short brim rolled up at the sides and flat at front and back; either blue or white covers could be worn. Enlisted ranks wore a wider-brimmed, softer 'pudding basin' hat similar to the early British model, with the brim turned up at the back and down at the front, and a dark blue ribbon tally with the gilt lettering 'U.S. NAVY'. The trade and rating badges worn on the left sleeve were the same as for male personnel.

There were four orders of dress for officers:

*Service Blue Dress, A:* —Navy blue jacket, skirt, and hat, black gloves and shoes. Navy blue or light blue shirt for working dress, white shirt and gloves for dress.

*Service Blue Dress, B:* —Identical but with white hat cover and gloves.

*Service White Dress:* —White jacket, skirt, long-sleeved shirt, shoes, gloves and hat cover.

*Working Dress:* —Navy blue jacket and skirt, white short-sleeved shirt, white gloves and hat cover.

The uniform jackets were single-breasted with four gilt buttons. The WAVE device, a foul anchor superimposed on a three-blade propeller, was attached to the rounded points of the collar. On the blue jacket the propeller was light blue and the anchor white, embroidered on a dark blue disc of

**Many American women joined non-military organizations to help their country's war effort. Here uniformed Civil Defence workers man a switchboard. (Lambert Studios)**

backing material. On the white jacket the propeller was dark blue, the anchor light blue, on a white backing. The ranking was rather similar to British practice, in light blue on the blue jacket and dark blue on the white jacket. Officers wore the cap badge of male officers, a gold national eagle over a silver shield over crossed anchors in gold on a dark blue backing. Chief petty officers wore a vertical gold foul anchor with the silver letters 'USN' across the shank, as their male counterparts.

Despite its similarity to that of male officers, this uniform, with the removal of gilt buttons and sleeve decorations, was virtually identical to civilian costumes of the day—with new buttons and a civilian hat it could be worn by any business woman.

Working overalls of blue cotton were issued to those working with aircraft; and a 'smock dress' of light blue could be worn over the uniform to protect it when any particular duty required it.

Slacks matching the jacket colours could be worn for duties where a skirt was considered impractical.

On 15 October 1943 the Bureau of Naval Personnel released a new set of Women's Reserve uniform regulations superseding those of March that year. The uniforms described were specifically forbidden to nurses. These revised instructions took account of the recent change in male officers' and enlisted men's dress, in that khaki had been replaced by slate grey. The new women's working uniform was therefore a pale grey cotton seersucker shirtwaist dress with a matching collarless jacket. The dress had a narrow collar with rounded points, worn folded over the jacket, which had lapels. The jacket was secured by four blue-black plastic buttons. The hat for enlisted ranks remained the same but with a pale grey cover. On the rounded ends of the lapels the WAVES device appeared on a circular backing $1\frac{1}{2}$in. in diameter. Black shoes and beige stockings were to be worn with the 'greys'.

New provisions were made in these regulations for the identification of female officers of the various staff corps. The insignia of the Hospital, Medical, Supply, Dental, and Civil Engineer Corps would now appear above the cuff rings of rank, but not in gilt in the male fashion. On the blue jacket and overcoat the oakleaves and caduceus were to be light blue and the acorns white. On the white and grey service jackets the oakleaves and caduceus were to be dark blue, the acorns light blue. A further change in regulations on 15 September 1944 granted line members of the Women's Reserve the star insignia worn by their male counterparts, in light blue on navy blue clothing and in navy blue on white and grey clothing.

The granting of relative rank in July 1942 was echoed in a uniform change of June 1944 affecting the Navy Nurse Corps. The Bureau of Naval Personnel ordered the removal of the 'NNC' cypher from the Corps device. The device of the anchor and oakleaf was now to be worn on the sleeve of the blue service coat in the same position as the star of line officers, and on the shoulder-boards of the white jacket. The cap badge became that of male officers. The Nurse Corps was now a component part of the regular Navy, and ranks were regularized along with insignia practice.

The superintendent, assistant superintendent, and so forth now gave way to Navy ranks up to and including captain, with the same sleeve lace and metal devices as worn by male officers.

*　　*　　*

Various modifications to women's uniforms in all the services occurred progressively throughout the war, too many to list in this book. In the WAC there was a general acceptance of the 'overseas' or 'garrison' sidecap; and the 1944 wool jacket modelled on British battledress, the 'Ike jacket', was taken into widespread use in many slightly varying forms. Women in uniform served overseas in many theatres of war, including the Mediterranean, the Pacific and CBI, and North-West Europe.

**American army nurses disembark in Normandy from an LCI. They wear combat clothing of 1943 pattern, webbing equipment and steel helmets, identical to the outfits issued to male GIs. (Imperial War Museum)**

# Germany

Long before the declaration of war the German authorities had laid down plans for the release of many male clerical staff for front line service. It was foreseen at the highest level that either the huge administrative 'tail' so essential for a modern army must be combed out drastically; or the numbers of men in combat units must be reduced by a significant factor. Neither solution appealed. It was necessary to obtain authorization from the government for the employment of women outside the frontiers of the Reich, and for the setting up of a formal, military-style organization to co-ordinate their contribution to the war effort, under conditions acceptable to all concerned. From this reserve pool could be recruited the Stabshelferinnen, who as their name suggests would in the first instance release large numbers of the military 'office personnel' for more active duties. Although the mobilization of women had already started by September 1939 it was as a direct result of the Russian campaign that by the end of 1941 much larger numbers of women were required.

Overall strengths of women involved directly in the war effort were, at the outbreak of war, some 140,000 in the Army, consisting of about 50,000 officials and 90,000 Helferinnen. In 1943–44 some 300,000 officials and Helferinnen were on the strength of the Reserve Army; in the same period some 8,000 Nachrichtenhelferinnen and 12,500 Stabshelferinnen were serving with the field army and in the occupied territories. The Luftwaffe had 130,000 women personnel. In the Kriegsmarine there were about 20,000 officials and Marinehelferinnen, mainly serving as office and communications staff.

The Helferinnen were essentially civil servants attached to the armed forces but without military status, although they were subject to military law and the Wehrmacht's disciplinary procedures. Many sub-divisions existed within the women's services, and they were not as neatly divided into women's arms of the army, navy and air force proper as was the case in Britain and America. Major branches were the Nachrichtenhelferinnen, which may be translated as 'communications assistants'; and the Luftwaffenhelferinnen, 'air force assistants', which included the Flugmeldedienst (air warning service) and Fernsprech- und Fernschreibbetriebsdienst (telephone and teletype services) and the Flakwaffenhelferinnen (air defence assistants). The navy and Waffen-SS both had parallel women's services employed in bureaucratic and communications duties. In fact the total numbers employed were small compared to the real requirements.

## Stabshelferinnen and Nachrichtenhelferinnen

The successful close of the French campaign in summer 1940 vastly increased the task of maintaining communications networks throughout the occupied West; and the German Red Cross offered the Wehrmacht many thousands of volunteer Helferinnen from their reserve to train as Nachrichtenhelferinnen. The training and reserve centre was at Giessen; coming under the authority of the Reserve Army, it was organized on entirely military lines and all training was supervised by male officers and NCOs. On all questions of welfare and working arrangements, however, the women personnel remained subject to their own officers and regulations. After training was completed, the Nachrichtenhelferinnen worked wherever possible under women officers and not alongside male personnel, and occupied their own barracks under female supervision, according to 'Heimordnung' regulations.

The army's Nachrichtenhelferinnen served throughout occupied Europe, suffering many privations as a result of wartime conditions. As representatives of the German way of life in a foreign country they were considered to be under the protection of German soldiers. Their reputation and welfare were mentioned in an OKW order to the effect that 'The soldiers' treatment of these German women must be the same as their conduct toward their own wives, mothers, sisters and daughters. It is a matter of honour for any decent German to behave correctly towards every German woman, especially those working alongside them in an enemy occupied country. Enemy propaganda has tried to besmirch the image of the Nachrichtenhelferinnen by spreading malicious gossip and evil rumours. With a whispering cam-

A damaged photograph, which nevertheless shows fairly clearly the uniform of the German Nachrichtenhelferinnen des Heeres. Note the unusual features of the jacket; see Plate G2. (Brian L. Davis)

paign the enemy has tried to represent these girls as unwomanly gun-toting Amazons. It is up to every German soldier to defend the honour of these girls. If a soldier humorously refers to the women as "Blitz Girls" there is nothing wrong with that; but if offensive remarks are passed, it is hoped that a more respectful comrade will object strongly. A German soldier has always been known for his chivalry, especially towards German women, and he who thinks otherwise is a scoundrel.' (The reference in this typically pompous exhortation to 'Blitz Girls' refers in a punning way to the lightning-bolt sleeve patch of the communications personnel, known as a 'blitz'.)

A major problem was the legal status of the Helferinnen in a war zone if taken prisoner, i.e. whether they would be treated as prisoners of war or partisans. Although working for the

1. Lance Corporal, ATS Provost, 1941
2. ATS Private, attached Royal Artillery, 1941
3. Polish ATS Driver, Ambulance Car Company

A

1. **ATS Corporal, Anti-Aircraft Command, 1940—41**
2. **WAAF Deputy Company Commander, 1940—41**
3. **WAAF Assistant Section Leader, 1940—41**

B

1. WRNS Despatch Rider
2. WRNS Third Officer
3. WRNS Signals Rating

C

1. WRNS Third Officer nursing sister, tropical dress
2. Lieutenant, US Navy Nurse Corps, 1944
3. Chief Nurse, US Navy Nurse Corps, 1943

D

1. 1st Class Petty Officer Yeoman, US Navy WAVES, 1943
2. Captain, US WAC; SHAEF, 1944
3. 2nd Lieutenant, US Marine Corps Womens' Reserves, 1944—45

1. Luftnachrichtenhelferin, spring 1941
2. Flakwaffenhelferin, 1944
3. Luftnachrichtenhelferin, 1942

F

1. Waffen-SS Helferin
2. Führerin, Stabshelferinnen
3. Italian MVSN Auxiliary, 'Aldo Resega' Brigade

G

1. Nurse, Soviet Army, 1941—43
2. Junior Lieutenant, Soviet Air Force, 1942
3. Yugoslav Partisan

armed services and wearing a uniform they were *not* women soldiers but were 'non-combatant in the armed forces' under the terms of the Hague Convention of 1907. These rights were extended to Helferinnen who eventually became prisoners of war after the invasion of France in 1944, irrespective of the fact that in the last few months of the war some did in fact take up arms. It should perhaps be noted here that in Russia, where the danger of sudden fluctuations in the front line and of partisan attack in rear areas was considerable, female personnel were largely concentrated within Army Group HQ areas.

The proper deployment of the Helferinnen was outlined in an order from OKW on 22 June 1942; 'In increasing numbers, women who are trained for office work, telephonists, etc. are needed especially in the areas outside the Reich, to replace soldiers who are urgently required for active service at the fronts. It is the will of the Führer that all German women who will be far from their homeland, helping the German armed forces, will be given every care and protection to make their tasks easier to accomplish. . . . On no account will they be involved in any type of military operation. A woman soldier does not belong to our Nationalistic idea of womanhood.'

At the beginning of 1942, those auxiliaries who were termed Stabshelferinnen—i.e. 'staff assistants' of various types not specifically serving with the communications branch—were being passed through training centres set up in Berlin (Centre III), Hartha-bei-Dresden (Centre IV) and Danzig (Centre XX). Here they were taught shorthand, typing, and military codes and procedures, with a final verbal examination which governed their placement in various groups and categories. Whilst their duties were often similar to those of the Nachrichtenhelferinnen, the Stabshelferinnen had different responsibilities. They worked under women officers in both military and civil service departments in the various occupied countries. The Stabshelferinnen-führerinnen (staff assistant leadership) were responsible to the staffs of the various Army Groups, and to Oberkommando des Heeres. They had an overall 'head', a Gebietsführerin, under direct command of OKH. In addition there were deputy heads responsible for their own particular

geographical areas—Bezirksführerinnen—who were directly answerable to the Gebietsführerin on matters directly concerned with running the women's service. A high-ranking civil servant of the German Women's Labour Service, with the title of Hauptführerin, was directly responsible for the affairs of the Stabshelferinnen to the Director General of the Ersatzheeres—the Reserve Army.

The West had top priority in the deployment of Stabshelferinnen from late 1941, with the bulk going to OKH, and the headquarters of Army Groups and Armies. With the progress of the campaign in the East, however, and the use of Poland as a major reinforcement and replacement staging area, the 'General Government' (as that unhappy nation was termed by the Germans) soon vied with France as the main area of employment

Three German army women auxiliaries pose for a photograph after being awarded the War Service Cross with Swords. All wear the silver and black 'blitz' tie brooch; the girl on the right can just be seen to wear the Stabshelferinnen des Heeres cuff title on the left sleeve above the buttoned tab. (Brian L. Davis)

25

**Nachrichtenhelferinnen des Heeres, wearing the mouse-grey smock-dress with a detachable white collar issued as a working overall. (Brian L. Davis)**

The Stabshelferinneneinsatz reached its maximum strength in the spring of 1944, but by this time the West was threatened with invasion and the East had already started a general retreat. Orders were rushed out to all women's service detachments serving outside the Reich, calling for their repatriation to the homeland. An OKW statement of November 1944 admitted that 'up to this date the whereabouts of many members of the Stabshelferinnen and Nachrichtenhelferinnen is still uncertain, especially in France. . . . It is thought that they frequently missed the timely orders to retreat. The number that returned from the south of France, and the number that were posted as missing, are indeterminable.'

The Nachrichtenhelferinnen and Stabshelferinnen wore almost identical uniforms; it appears that the main difference lay in the use of a green-on-grey Gothic-lettered cuff title on the left forearm by the latter. The normal service dress consisted of a sidecap, double-breasted jacket and skirt in field grey; the exact shade seems to have varied widely, as with all 'field grey' uniforms. The cap was cut like an army *Feldmütze*, with a deep turn-up 'scooped' low at the front. A small version of the army's eagle and swastika insignia was sewn to the turn-up at the front—the Reichs cockade was not worn. The jacket was of unusual shape. Four dark grey-green plastic composition buttons were set on the double-breasted front. The collar had deep notched lapels. There were two internal breast pockets, with external pointed flaps fastened by buttons; but on the right flap, on which no button was visible, the army's eagle badge was worn. There were two internal pockets set on the ribs, with flapless vertical openings closed centrally by visible buttons. The cuffs were decorated with buttoned tabs on the outside of the sleeve, the ends being three-pointed. The skirt had two frontal pleats.

The shirt-blouse was either white, for summer 'walking out', or mouse-grey, both being worn with a conventional black necktie. The shoes were laced, of black leather. In winter grey stockings were worn; in some summer dress orders, white ankle socks replaced these. There was a grey working 'smock-dress' with a detachable white collar, and a white summer equivalent. All these orders of dress may be found in the accompanying

of these staff assistants. On 12 September 1942 an OKH order instructed that those Stabshelferinnen who had served over one year in France were to be exchanged for those serving a similar period in the East—an order reflecting the relative popularity of the postings, no doubt, and the need to maintain morale among the assistants serving under the harsher conditions of Poland.

Apart from France, the Low Countries and Norway, the Stabshelferinnen were also posted as the war progressed to the Balkans, Greece and —after the take-over of Italy by the Germans in 1943—to northern Italy. Other small groups were despatched to Finland. In these areas they came directly under OKW command. Apart from the administrative personnel there were accounts workers, drivers, translators, and so forth, recruited to the level of requirements of the Army group concerned. By the end of 1942 there was an urgent need for translators, recruited mainly from Russian émigrées and from German Baltic refugees who had a working knowledge of Russian. These volunteers were trained at Hartha-bei-Dresden under army command.

photographs. Qualified communications personnel—i.e. all Nachrichtenhelferinnen and many Stabshelferinnen—wore on the tie a large, round enamel brooch in black with silver edging and a silver 'blitz'. The other insignia of rank and trade were worn as follows.

Rank titles were subject to change during the war, and bore only an approximate relationship to conventional military ranks. They were divided into grades roughly equivalent to privates and corporals — Helferinnen, Oberhelferinnen and Haupthelferinnen; grades equivalent to sergeants and senior NCOs—Truppführerinnen, and Obertruppführerinnen; and those approximating officers' ranks from Leutnant to Oberstleutnant, which were respectively Dienstführerin, Oberdienstführerin, Hauptdienstführerin (equivalent to company officer ranks), Stabsführerin and Oberstabsführerin (equivalent to field ranks). These titles will sometimes be found without the word 'dienst', e.g. Oberführerin, equivalent to Oberleutnant.

The junior grades wore the eagle insignia on cap and right breast pocket flap in white thread on dark green backing. There was no piping on cap or collar. The grade of Vorhelferin, equivalent to the army's Oberschütze or senior private, and a grade which did not remain in currency throughout the war, was marked by a silver four-point 'pip' or star on a dark green disc on the left upper sleeve. The Oberhelferin wore a single silver-grey chevron on the usual dark green triangle, and the Haupthelferin wore the chevron with a pip in the centre of the backing. All these grades wore the 'blitz' in yellow on a green oval backing patch on the left sleeve, above any ranking.

Both 'sergeant' grades, collectively termed Unterführerinnen, seem to have worn two pips on the centre of the backing to the single chevron. They had black and yellow mixed piping on the crown seam and the front 'scoop' of the sidecap; silver-thread-on-green eagle insignia on cap and breast; and the 'blitz' arm badge in silver, with the patch edged in silver cord.

Führerinnen appear to have worn the same eagle, arm patch and piping as the above, but without arm chevrons. Oberführerinnen are listed as wearing silver cap piping, silver cap and breast eagles on green, silver piping round the

upper part of the collar, and black patches in the corners of the upper lapels surrounded at outside and bottom edges with a short 'L' of silver *Tresse* braid. The silver 'blitz', patch edged silver, was worn on the sleeve. Hauptführerinnen wore the same but with a silver pip on the black collar patches. Stabsführerinnen wore gold cap and collar piping; gold-on-green eagles on cap and breast; gold *Tresse* on the collar patch; and the green sleeve patch had a gold 'blitz' and gold edging. Oberstabsführerinnen wore the same but with a gold pip on the collar patches.

## Luftnachrichtenhelferinnen

Although in peacetime the various departments of the Wehrmacht naturally had some women employees, they were no more involved with the operational side than the female employees of the

The white summer working dress of the Nachrichtenhelferinnen, fastened at the throat with the 'blitz' brooch normally worn on the necktie. The trade patch on the upper left arm is in the same colours as on the grey jacket. Note white ankle socks. (Brian L. Davis)

Hilf siegen
## als Luftnachrichtenhelferin
Auskunft erteilt jede Luftwaffendienststelle

**Poster appealing for recruits for the Luftnachrichtenhelferinnen, 1941.**

general civil service of other countries. With the outbreak of war the Luftwaffe, in particular, experienced a great need for women personnel in the communications, telephone and telegraph, and air warning systems, where they worked alongside male technicians. As war pushed the defensible boundaries of the Reich outwards, they too moved into the occupied territories in the same way as their army counterparts.

The main branch of the Luftwaffenhelferinnen-schaft were the Luftnachrichtenhelferinnen, or 'air communications assistants'. These were divided between the Flugmeldedienst (air warning service) and the telephone and teletype service.

The growing pressure of Allied air raids led in October 1943 to the formation of the Flakwaffen-helferinnenkorps. Most were volunteers from the general labour pool of the Luftwaffenhelferinnen,

but in emergencies the local labour directorate could draft civilian personnel proper into the service. Always stationed on Reich territory, they operated listening devices and searchlights, radar apparatus, and other equipment used by the air defence forces. In the last year of the war women increasingly took over male duties on gun sites, actually manning flak batteries in action.

The responsibilities of the Luftwaffenhelferinnen in general expanded as the war continued and the shortage of manpower became acute. Apart from the need for aircrew, the Luftwaffe was also combed out to provide men for the air force combat divisions, the Luftwaffenfeld-divisionen; and late in 1944 the women's service was required to provide an additional 70,000 personnel as quickly as possible. This was achieved in the spring of 1945. The total number of women serving with the Luftwaffe was, as already stated, some 130,000 at peak strength.

The uniform of the air force female auxiliaries was a sidecap, a single-breasted jacket and a pleated skirt in Luftwaffe blue-grey. The cap was of Luftwaffe shape, that is the turn-up was cut evenly all round without a frontal 'scoop'. The jacket had a broad, notched collar and lapels, three blue-black plastic buttons down the front, and two internal side pockets with straight external flaps fastened by concealed buttons. The shirt-blouse was either white (summer 'walking out') or light blue (service dress), with a black necktie. Black laced shoes were worn.

The use of insignia was complex and subject to several changes. The titles for the various grades were also extremely confusing, changing several times and being different in prefix for the different branches; e.g. in the air warning service the junior rank of Helferin (early 1940) became in August 1940 'Flugmeldehelferin', in February 1941 'Luftnachrichten-Flugmeldehelferin', and in July 1941 reverted to 'Flugmeldehelferin'. The basic sequence for the Luftnachrichtenhelferinnen was as follows:

Prior to June 1940, ranking was as standard Luftwaffe male issue. From June 1940 to July 1941 ranking was worn on both cuffs of the jacket. The most junior grade, Anwärterin, which wore no insignia, disappeared from August 1940. The Helferin wore a single horizontal silver braid bar approximately 3 in. long by ½ in. deep. The Auf-sicht (after August 1940, Aufsicht-Helferin) wore the same with a single four-point silver thread pip centrally above it. The Betriebsgruppenführerin (after August 1940, Betriebsgruppenunterfüh-rerin) wore two pips over the bar. The Haupt-gruppenführerin (after August 1940, Betriebs-gruppenführerin und Heimleiterin) wore three pips over a bar.

In July 1941 a further order instituted a ranking system which lasted for the rest of the war. A series of simple, rather shallow, point-downwards silver braid chevrons were worn on the upper left arm, with 'officers' from Führerin upwards having a round 'curl' in the bottom chevron in naval style. The ranks and insignia were:

| | | |
|---|---|---|
| Helferin | ... | One plain chevron |
| Oberhelferin | ... | Two plain chevrons |
| Haupthelferin | ... | Three plain chevrons |
| Führerin | ... | One chevron with a curl |
| Oberführerin | ... | One plain above one with a curl |
| Hauptführerin | ... | Two plain above one with a curl |
| Stabsführerin | ... | Three plain above one with a curl |

Grades from Führerin up also wore a four-point silver pip or star on each upper lapel of the jacket and greatcoat. From October 1943 the upper part of their collar and lapels were piped silver, as was the upper edge of the cap turn-up. Previously all grades had worn golden-brown *Waffenfarbe* piping in this position, and 'non-commissioned' grades continued to do so.

From November 1940 the Luftwaffe eagle and swastika insignia, in pale grey on dark blue for junior ranks and in silver on dark blue for Führerin and upwards, was worn on the right breast of the jacket and, small, on the front of the crown of the sidecap. The Reich cockade was not worn. All grades seem to have worn a tiny silver stickpin in the shape of a Luftwaffe eagle on the black necktie. 'Trade' patches, indicating qualifications and functions, were worn in white on round blue-grey patches 12 cm below the shoulder seam of the left sleeve; rank chevrons were worn 1 cm below this. The normal patch seen in photographs is that of radio operator, featuring an 'X'-shaped bundle of

lightnings spreading from a central, horizontal, stylized pair of oakleaves (see Plate F1). Teletype operators wore a single pair of jagged lightnings, with small arrowheads at the bottom, arranged in a saltire. Telephone operators had two light-nings entwined, giving the effect of an angular figure '8' or two flat diamonds one above the other, with four arrowheads pointing off to the corners from the central top and bottom points of the diamonds. Signals personnel attached to the flying and flak branches wore a conventional 'blitz' patch, as illustrated on Plate F3. Towards the end of the war a wide range of trade patches associated with flak duties would have been seen in use by women.

Positions of command, as opposed to actual grades within the service, were marked by 5 mm aluminium braid stripes around the cuffs of the jacket, greatcoat and working smock, 12 cm from the bottom of the sleeve. Grades in charge of a *Betriebszug* wore one stripe, and grades in charge of a *Betriebskameradschaft* wore two. (The basic unit of one Haupthelferin and up to eight Hel-ferinnen was termed an *Ln-H-Betriebsgruppe*. Two to four *Gruppen* made up a *Betriebszug*, normally commanded by a Führerin; and two to four *Züge* made up a *Betriebskameradschaft*, normally commanded by an Oberführerin.)

**Group of Luftnachrichtenhelferinnen manning a switch-board, some time between July 1941, when this type of arm ranking came into use, and October 1943, after which the Führerin—in the centre—would have silver collar piping. Note trade patches of Flugmelde (air raid warning) per-sonnel, worn by girl on right; and qualified telephone opera-tor, worn by the Führerin in the centre. The latter also has the single silver command stripe around her cuffs, described in the text. (Brian L. Davis)**

**Flakwaffenhelferin, 1944, manning a searchlight battery. The cap, jacket and thin sleeve chevron of grade can all be seen. (Brian L. Davis)**

## Flakwaffenhelferinnen

Flakwaffenhelferinnen, mobilized in late 1943, wore a uniform in keeping with their more strenuous outdoor duties. The headgear was the *Einheitsfeldmütze* or 'M1943 cap' as it is sometimes termed today, with the turn-up fastened at the front with a single button. The cap was in Luftwaffe blue-grey, and bore the Luftwaffe eagle badge on the front of the crown. A single-breasted jacket rather similar to the airman's *Fliegerbluse*, with a folded-open collar, fly front, and no visible breast pockets, was fastened by a narrow cloth belt with a metal 'stirrup' buckle. Two side pockets of patch type had buttoned, rectangular flaps with rounded corners. Slacks were normally worn—like the jacket, in Luftwaffe blue-grey—with heavy black laced shoes. The badge of the Flakwaffenhelferinnen was worn on the right upper sleeve—a white outline shield of heater shape, with a white vertical broadsword point down within it, and a white Luftwaffe eagle and swastika over all.

The ranking system worn by the Flakwaffen-

helferinnen was the same as that to which all Luftwaffenhelferinnen who had *not* been subject to the previous regulations for Nachrichtenhelferinnen (listed above) changed from March 1944. It was built up from the same elements—shallow, silver braid chevrons, point down on the upper left arm, with a curl in the bottom chevron for grades from Führerin upwards:

| Lw-Helferinnen | Flakw-Helferinnen | |
| --- | --- | --- |
| Helferin | Helferin | One plain thin chevron |
| Oberhelferin | Oberhelferin | Two plain thin chevrons |
| Haupthelferin | Truppführerin* | One plain thin chevron below one thick chevron |
| Führerin | Führerin | One thin chevron with curl below two thick chevrons |
| Oberführerin | Oberführerin | Two thick chevrons above one thin plain above one thin with curl |
| Hauptführerin | Hauptführerin | Two thick above two thin plain above one thin with curl |
| Stabsführerin | Stabsführerin | Three thick chevrons above one thin with curl |
| Oberstabsführerin | Oberstabsführerin | Three thick above one thin plain above one thin with curl |

*Between Truppführerin and Führerin, the Flakwaffenhelferinnen had the rank of Obertruppführerin, identified by one thick over two thin, plain chevrons.

Ranks from Führerin and up, in both services, were marked by silver piping round the collar and upper lapel and a silver pip on both upper collar points.

## Nursing Services

Other female services were the Schwestern- und Betreuungshelferinnen, the nurses and welfare workers. The Wehrmacht had no integral corps of female nurses for the military sick and wounded, and these were provided by the same organizations which had come forward in the First World War: groups of nurses from convents, from the German Red Cross (DRK) and from voluntary organizations. Combined under the title Schwesternhelferinnen, they received the conscript's rate of pay, and staffed both rear and relatively frontline hospitals. Initially the OKH had very limited powers over these establishments. With the expansion of the war it was necessary for the military to take over this organization, and from 1943 the whole of the female staffs were separated from the DRK and formed into Betreuungshelferinnen, coming under OKH authority.

Due to the proximity to the front line in which many of these nurses worked, their casualties were quite high, but records are only fragmentary. The same is in fact true of the casualties among all German women's services; due to the conditions of the defeat of the Third Reich, such documentation as was ever gathered has largely disappeared. We know only that casualties were high in 1944–45, and that several thousands of women disappeared into the chaos of defeat and were never satisfactorily accounted for.

## RAD, Kriegshilfsdienst, and Luftwaffeneinsatz

The picture of several different and independent organizations for women, none of them strictly speaking a part of the armed forces, becomes further complicated with the arrival on the scene of the RAD—the Reichs Labour Service. The only exception to Germany's lack of a general registration of women for war service was the call-up of several age groups between seventeen and 45 for the women's Arbeitsdienst, from which were later formed the Kriegshilfsdienst and Luftwaffeneinsatz. These should not be confused with those army and air force auxiliary organizations already described.

In summer 1941 women's service in the RAD was extended from six to twelve months, and the additional period was to be served in the Kriegshilfsdienst, in munitions or ordnance factories, in stores, in communications centres and hospitals, or in general duties for the Wehrmacht. This extension of service helped raise the strength of the female RAD—RADw—to 150,000 by 1942.

The Kriegshilfsdienst—literally, 'War Help Service'—was not a single auxiliary, but was made up of several groups under the direction of women holding the rank of Reichsarbeitsführerin. The various groups of Kriegshilfsdienstmädchen were supposed to work and live as directed by the authorities, but the problems of finding suitable accommodation near their scattered work places, of providing allowances, and of placing the right girls in the right jobs were never really solved. The training periods for some office jobs proved too

short; and the period of service was so short that a girl would just become valuable in her job, and would then have to be replaced by an inexperienced one. Most employing authorities refused to accept them unless they agreed to serve for longer than their statutory six months, and this further complicated the administration. Later in the war the Kriegshilfsdienst concentrated on the armament industry, solving some of their problems by building barracks for the girls at the required sites.

One branch of the RADw Kriegshilfsdienst was the Luftwaffeneinsatz—it is important to remember that this remained a part of the RADw, and it should not be confused with the Luftwaffenhelferinnen, Flakwaffenhelferinnen or Nachrichtenhelferinnen already described, although the women from all these organizations worked side by side.

Initially the Luftwaffeneinsatz provided about 4,000 women who worked in the air communications and air raid warning services. In the latter service they slowly took over more responsibility for radar work; and about 13,000 were working in the Flugmeldedienst alone by the end of the war. A small number of these RADw girls worked in the Jägerleitstellen (fighter direction stations) of the air defence network, on a basis of careful individual selection; they were considered a great success.

From the spring of 1944 the RADw women became more and more involved with the duties of the home defence flak batteries. The male officers and NCOs and male gunlayers were supported by women who took over all other duties; the proportion of women 'gunners' obviously varied from battery to battery, depending upon availability of trained personnel. By the spring of 1945 the flak branch of the Kriegshilfsdienst rose to a strength of about 25,000, and from January 1945 it was ordered that they should take over the running of searchlight batteries entirely. Although some women were already serving with the searchlights, and although 30,000 in all were earmarked for the take-over, in fact only a relatively small proportion of the 300 or so functional batteries could be taken over by women before the end of the war, due to the general breakdown in administration and training.

**Group of Flakwaffenhelferinnen on searchlight battery duty, 1944; note slacks tucked into socks and heavy laced shoes. (Brian L. Davis)**

At the end of the war it was decided that the final barriers must be swept away, and that the women of the Kriegshilfsdienst Luftwaffeneinsatz must take over direct military duties from male soldiers. In November 1944 the women who had already volunteered for a limited service period were compulsorily conscripted to serve for the duration of the war; their 'head start' in training made them more valuable then the newly conscripted women. In all, the compulsory call-up of women for the Luftwaffeneinsatz brought in between 300,000 and 350,000; the high proportion of college students in this group, as well as the core of trained 'volunteers', considerably eased one problem which had dogged the Kriegshilfsdienst, and which would seem inseparable from the chaotic lack of co-ordination in mobilizing women's services which characterized the Ger-

man experience—the problem of a chronic shortage of potential leaders. Although it took longer to train women for positions of leadership and technical responsibility in the air defences than in any other duties, and although the start of a major effort had been left far too late, there was now some improvement.

## The Wehrmachtshilferinnenkorps
In the final months of the war there occurred one of those great 'paper' upheavals in the organization of the German services which so characterized the last days of the Nazis. Grandiose new expedients would be announced, detailed down to the last bureaucratic scruple, which would in fact bear very little relationship to the reality of a collapsing Reich and which would actually be implemented on only the most fragmentary basis.

An order of 25 July 1944, from Hitler through Goebbels, and significantly only days after the shaken Führer had been picked out of the rubble left by the generals' bomb attack, called for the formation of a 'Wehrmachtshilferinnenkorps'. Broadly, the purpose of this new organization was to embrace and rationalize under central control and co-ordination the existing, fragmented women's services; and to mobilize all available women, compulsorily, without the prior training requirements or restrictions which had hitherto applied, in order to free for front line service every possible German soldier.

A considerable effort was made to put this order into effect, but its administrative detail need not concern us here, since it came to very little in practical terms before Germany's final collapse.

It is, finally, quite interesting to note that in February and March of 1945 Hitler apparently abandoned his previous prejudice against the idea of armed women soldiers. By the end of February he had authorized the trial formation of a female battalion; possibly this was seen more as a piece of internal propaganda, to inspire the men to greater efforts, than as a serious military expedient. But in March an OKW order cancelled all previous orders on the subject of firearms for women; these would not now be issued except to special categories such as flak crews and those on guard duties.

# Russia

While our detailed knowledge of the Russian armed forces is much more limited than in the case of the Western nations, it was in the Soviet forces that women crossed the last barrier, and formed actual combat units. The staggering losses suffered by the USSR throughout the war, and particularly in the first six months of unbroken German victories, caused such a desperate shortage of personnel of every type that the distinction between the sexes was quickly abandoned. At first women served in non-combatant rôles— the usual medical, communications, transport, and logistic duties common to all women's services. But the continuing heavy losses brought them right into the front line, weapon in hand, by mid-1942, and they continued to fight right through the war. It is not thought that actual units of conventional combat infantry were formed from women recruits and put into the line; but women served in a wide range of capacities in all the technical branches, including the artillery, and served as combat aircrew and tank crews. A few brief examples must suffice to represent the major contribution the women of Russia made to Soviet, and thus to Allied victory in 1945. Apart from women serving at the front, it is worth recording that women came to represent fully half of the labour force in the factories feeding the Soviet armies. There was no systematic conscription of women for the armed forces; but so total was the disruption of all normal life in the USSR, and so high the proportion of civilians brought brutally into contact with the fighting, that government appeals for volunteers for the 'Great Patriotic War' found a ready response.

Most women combat aircrew served with the all-female 122nd Air Group of the Soviet Air Force. Formed at Engels on the Volga as early as October 1941, the fighter component of this group was the 586th Fighter Air Regiment, commanded by Major Tamara Alexandrovna Kazarinova. Flying Yak-1, Yak-7B and Yak-9 single-seat, single-engined fighters, the regiment flew a total of 4,419 operational sorties, took part in 125 air combats, and was credited with 38 confirmed aerial victories. The other components of the 122nd Group were the 587th Bomber and 588th Night Bomber Air Regiments. The night bombers were initially antiquated biplanes and other obsolete types deemed unable to survive in the dangerous daytime skies. Their crews flew hair-raising night missions at low level over enemy front lines, with only the most rudimentary of equipment and aids.

The appearance of women in mainly male units was taken much more for granted in the Soviet forces than in the West; and in fact the USSR's top-scoring woman pilot served in a mixed unit, the 73rd Guards Fighter Air Regiment. She was Junior Lieutenant Lydia Litvak, a Yak pilot who was credited with twelve confirmed 'kills' before her death in action on 1 August 1943. In all, 30 Soviet airwomen were awarded the coveted Gold Star of a Hero of the Soviet Union.

Russian tank crews were recruited initially from men with experience of driving and maintaining trucks and agricultural tractors, and who thus did not have to be trained absolutely from scratch. The hideous losses suffered by the armoured troops in 1941 and 1942 depleted this pool of semi-trained men; and in 1943 women began to arrive at the front as drivers in tank brigades. They had already played an important rôle behind the lines as test drivers and delivery crews at the tank factories and railheads; this experience in fact

**Moscow women undergoing training in reserve formations —local militias, known as *apolchenie* or DNO units. They wear an assortment of military and civilian dress and rudimentary equipment; some at the rear of this column carry the old 7.62mm Moysin-Nagant rifle. (Novosti)**

gave them a more thorough grounding in their trade than many of the hastily trained young men who were being drafted to the front. The women volunteers were transferred from the factories for combat training in small groups throughout 1944 and 1945, and by VE Day some had risen to be tank commanders.

A famous woman tanker was Sergeant Maria Oktyabr'skaya, who was posthumously awarded the Order of Lenin. In 1941 this woman of Crimean peasant stock, 39 years old, was working as a telephone operator; her husband was a commissar with an artillery unit, and was killed that year in the German invasion. She saved her wages towards subscribing to public funds to pay for a tank, a popular gesture in Russia at that time; and went to work in an armaments factory. It was while working in this Siberian factory that she volunteered for training as a tank mechanic. In October 1943 she was assigned as driver, with the rank of sergeant, to the T-34 tank commanded by Lieutenant Petr Chebotko, a troop leader in a Guards tank brigade.

Oktyabr'skaya first saw action at Novoye Selo in the Vitebsk sector, where, in November 1943, she destroyed a German anti-tank gun by running it over. On 17 January 1944 her T-34 Model 43, a presentation vehicle from subscribers in the Sverdlovsk area named 'Boyevaya Podruga' ('Fighting Friend'), was knocked out by a mine; she received severe injuries, and died in March. Her exploits were publicized; and it is pleasant to record that a subscription tank bearing her slogan 'Boyevaya Podruga', a heavy IS-2 model, was present at the taking of Berlin.

Russian servicewomen wore exactly the same uniforms and insignia as their male counterparts, apart from the use of khaki (sometimes dark blue) skirts with service dress. For reasons of space we must direct interested readers to standard works of uniform reference, rather than trying to précis Red Army dress regulations in their entirety.

## Underground Movements

Apart from service in the conventional forces, thousands of Russian women travelled and fought with the partisan groups which infested the German-held areas of Russia. The terrain was too vast and too primitive for any army to police it effectively; and with tens of thousands of Soviet troops cut off and scattered behind the front lines during the lightning German advances of 1941, the formation of a very effective partisan network was only a matter of time. In this savage war of raids and reprisals many civilians became involved, and often their only hope of survival was to join a partisan band. Women played a full part, not only as messengers, quartermasters and nurses, but also as scouts, snipers, explosives experts, radio operators, and undercover agents.

It need hardly be stressed that the same story could be told of the women of all the occupied nations. Prized by underground movements for their ability to merge with the population at large, women were invaluable agents and supporters of all these organizations; they took the same terrible risks as their menfolk, and all too often suffered the same hideous fate. They were particularly visible in their contribution to the success of Tito's partisan army in Yugoslavia, where girls, often only teenagers, played a major part in the communications network on which this uniquely successful guerilla general depended for the intelligence which kept him one jump ahead of the enemy forces of occupation, and of his Chetnik rivals.

# The Plates

*A1: Britain: Lance Corporal, ATS Provost*
The basic ATS uniform bears Military Police embellishments, including the use of the male peaked khaki cap with a stiff top, in order to take the red crown cover of the MPs. The cap badge carries the ATS cypher, the shoulder-straps the same cypher without the crowned wreath. The shoulder-titles read ATS PROVOST in dark blue on red, and a dark red and blue lanyard is worn on the right shoulder to the breast pocket. Note the whistle chain. The red-on-dark-blue MP brassard is exactly the same as that worn by male personnel; so, of course, is the ranking chevron.

*A2: Britain: ATS Private, attached Royal Artillery, walking-out dress*
The privately purchased forage cap is in the

colours of the arm of service to which this girl is attached—the dark blue and red of the artillery, whose bomb-and-scroll badge is also worn on the left breast. The shoulder-titles and cap badge are the same as for the previous figure. Like all personnel of the day, she carries a gasmask in the standard khaki webbing satchel.

*A3: Poland, ATS Driver, Ambulance Car Company*
Similar to the uniform of a British ATS officer, this tunic has 'bellows' pockets in the skirts, and is of superior material. Note two small brass buttons at the rear edge of the cuff. The bronze cap and collar badges show a cross within a circular rim; the white-on-crimson national shoulder titles were common to all Polish personnel, with silver lettering for officers. The national cap badge, the silver eagle and Amazon shield, is worn here on the left breast. The cap, all in khaki cloth with a soft ruched crown, a chinstrap and neckpiece both worn up, is standard ATS issue. A small leather pouch closed by a brass stud is worn on the right side of the belt.

*B1: Britain: ATS Corporal, Anti-Aircraft Command*
The issue steel helmet, painted khaki green, was worn by personnel in exposed action stations—

Posed photograph showing a Red Army nurse towing a wounded man off the battlefield by means of a strap. Though posed, it shows a procedure often carried out under fire by Soviet nurses; and the girl herself, named as Yelena Koval-chuk, wears the Order of the Red Banner for valour. Photographed in summer 1942, she wears typically plain pre-1943 field dress—khaki *pilotka* cap with red star badge, and khaki *rubaha* shirt-tunic with breast pockets and fall collar. (Novosti)

and gun sites on RAF operational fields certainly qualified for that description in 1940–41. Battle-dress blouse and full-cut slacks were also worn when working on the gun and searchlight sites, with the leather trench jerkin in cold weather. The sheepskin mitten is taken from a photograph, and its odd back pad is unexplained. The shoulder-patch of AA Command appears on both sleeves, as do the standard rank chevrons in pale khaki herringbone pattern on a khaki backing.

*B2: Britain: WAAF Deputy Company Commander*
This rank, equivalent to an RAF Flying Officer, was changed to 'Section Officer' in 1942. The officers' cap has a cloth-covered peak and the RAF officers' cap badge in gold, silver and red on a black backing. The 'A' for Auxiliary is worn on the upper collar points in brass; the only other insignia is the ranking, a single pale-blue-on-dark-blue sleeve ring. 'Bellows' skirt pockets identify an officer's tunic. The cap is the same basic shape as that of the ATS but has a black mohair band and a black leather chinstrap.

*B3: Britain: WAAF Assistant Section Leader*
Conventional corporal's stripes identify this pre-1942 rank. The albatross shoulder-badge of all non-commissioned personnel of the RAF and WAAF surmounts the 'A' of Auxiliary, both in pale blue thread on midnight blue backing, like the chevrons. In contrast to the officer she wears a cap with a brass WAAF cap badge, and a black leather peak; the tunic also lacks the external skirt pockets. Army khaki webbing gasmask satchels were often worn in the RAF. The steel helmet, however, has been painted grey-blue.

*C1: Britain: WRNS Despatch Rider*
The dark blue peaked cap has a full earflap drop, fastened under the chin here. The goggles are the well-known cellophane 'gas goggles'. Interestingly, the reefer jacket is single-breasted here; it is worn without insignia, and with dark blue breeches reinforced with khaki, black buckled leggings, and black shoes.

*C2: Britain: WRNS Third Officer*
The RN officer's cap badge in gold, silver and red is worn on the black mohair band of the dark blue

tricorn hat. The reefer jacket has eight brass buttons, the top one being left unfastened. A white handkerchief is worn in the slit pocket on the left breast. The insignia of this junior commissioned rank is worn in light blue on each sleeve.

## C3: Britain: WRNS Signals Rating
Her rating is indicated by the 'bunting tosser's' sleeve badge of crossed blue and white flags, and by her cap tally—HMS *Mercury* was the home base for communications training. She wears the 1942 regulation 'sailor's cap' with a white summer top.

## D1: Britain: WRNS Third Officer nursing sister, tropical dress
The 'pudding basin' type hat was favoured for tropical uniform, worn with the black band and coloured officers' cap badge of the European uniform hat. The ranking was worn on dark blue shoulder-boards in gold. The white short-sleeved dress, worn with white shoes and stockings, had a cloth belt with a concealed crossover fastening.

## D2: USA: Lieutenant, US Navy Nurse Corps, 1944
The slate-grey 'overseas cap' and dress of the 1944 uniform regulations replaced the earlier pattern in light khaki material, for summer or tropical wear. The double-breasted dress has four blue-black buttons, two more on the crossover cloth belt, and a slit pocket on the left breast. Black shoes, short grey gloves, and a black shoulder-bag were the normal accessories. The cap bears the gilt Nurse Corps insignia on the left and the silver bars of a naval lieutenant on the right; they are both repeated on the collar.

## D3: USA: Chief Nurse, US Navy Nurse Corps, 1943
At this date ranks had yet to be standardized between male and female personnel; this grade was equivalent to Lieutenant (junior grade), and the single silver bar of that rank is worn on the right shirt collar. The Nurse Corps oakleaf and anchor insignia in gilt is worn as a crown badge on the white-topped cap, with its gilt chinstrap mounted at the top edge of the black mohair band. The Corps badge is repeated on the left shirt collar. The stripe-and-a-half of this rank is worn in gold on the shoulder-boards.

## E1: USA: 1st Class Petty Officer Yeoman, WAVES, 1943
The light grey 1943 working uniform, with matching hat. The collarless jacket is worn over the dress, both in pale grey seersucker material; note black bow tie under collar of dress, and WAVES badges on lapels of jacket—a foul anchor in bright 'Reserve' blue on a dark blue propeller. The rating and specialty badge is worn on the left sleeve only—the eagle and three chevrons separated in this case by crossed quills—in dark blue.

## E2: USA: Captain, WAC, SHAEF, 1944
By this stage the Women's Army Corps had begun to accept the 'overseas cap' as a replacement for the képi, and officers could sometimes be seen in this more flattering headgear, with the mixed gold and black piping of commissioned rank, and their rank insignia on the left side. The 1944 'Ike jacket', which like the cap is in a brownish 'Olive Drab', varied in many small details of pockets, buttons, etc., especially among officers. It was unusual, but by no means unknown, to see the Olive Drab officer's cuff braid from the four-pocket service tunic worn on the 'Ike'. Silver bars of rank appear on both shoulder-straps; brass cut-out US cyphers on each upper lapel; and the brass Athena's head on each lower lapel. Shirt, tie and skirt are all in a light khaki shade—comparable to an officer's 'pink' slacks. Gold bars indicate overseas service, six months per bar, on the left forearm. The shoulder-patch is that of Supreme Headquarters Allied Expeditionary Force, where many WACs were employed. The shoulder-bag, beige stockings and brown, buckled shoes are all regulation.

## E3: USA: Second Lieutenant, USMC Women's Reserve, 1944-45
The officers' white summer service dress, in seersucker material, had four patch pockets with pointed flaps, and dark green plastic buttons. The jacket had an open collar with bronze USMC 'collar dogs', and short sleeves. The jaunty cap, and the detachable shoulder-boards, were in a grass green cloth. The former had the bronze USMC insignia on the crown above white cords, and the latter bore ranking at the outer end— here, a single gold bar. Beige stockings, white

shoes, and a shoulder-bag similar to that of E2 but with a green cloth cover, completed the outfit.

*F1: Germany: Luftnachrichtenhelferin, spring 1941*
The cap, skirt, dark grey stockings and shoes would be the same as those worn by F3. Since November 1940 the Luftwaffe breast eagle was worn; and note the necktie pin in the same shape. The ranking of Betriebsgruppenunterführerin is worn on the cuff, in the pre-July 1941 style; and as yet there is no silver collar piping, although from this rank upwards the silver 'pip' is worn on

A Red Army woman officer in the uniform of 1943–45: the *rubaha* acquired a stand collar without patches but with two small buttons; rank and arm-of-service was indicated on traditional shoulder-boards; the front buttons became visible; and breast pockets were worn only by officers. The field shoulder-boards were in khaki cloth, edged and lined with the arm-of-service colour—here, apparently, the red of the infantry, who normally did not wear an identifying badge on the shoulder-board in the manner of other branches. The rank is Senior Lieutenant, indicated by one central red line and three silver stars. Decorations are, on her right breast, the Orders of the Red Star and the Patriotic War, above the Guards unit badge; and on her left breast the Gold Star of a Hero of the Soviet Union, above the Order of Lenin and what appear to be two separate awards of the Order of the Red Banner, above the medal for the Defence of the Caucasus. (Imperial War Museum)

the rounded upper points. The 'trade' patch is that of a qualified radio NCO—geprüfter Funk-unteroffizier.

*F2: Germany: Flakwaffenhelferin, 1944*
The peaked field cap bears the Luftwaffe eagle but no cockade; the eagle is repeated on the breast, and the insignia of this organization is worn on the right upper arm. The two thin silver braid chevrons of an Oberhelferin balance it on the left sleeve. Note the jacket, rather similar to the male *Flieger-bluse*, with a piece of black ribbon in the collar buttonhole signifying a relative recently killed. The slacks are tucked into heavy socks, and thick-soled laced black shoes are worn; this organization operated in the open air, on rather more strenuous duties than the Nachrichtenhelferinnen.

*F3: Germany: Luftnachrichtenhelferin, 1942*
The three chevrons of a Haupthelferin are worn on the left arm only, below the 'blitz' patch of signals personnel working with the flying branch. Note golden-brown piping on the turn-up of the *Fliegermütze*. The jacket is fastened with three blue-black plastic pierced buttons, but the side pocket flaps have concealed buttons.

*G1: Germany: SS-Helferin, Reichsschule staff*
Photographs show a rather unusual sidecap with no turn-up and a high ridged crown, bearing the SS eagle and swastika; the cap seems to be a darker shade of field grey than the jacket and skirt. The former resembles the Luftwaffe women's jacket in cut, but with pointed upper collar piped silver, and a left breast pocket. No information on rank insignia has been published, and the several surviving photographs show no differences between the girls illustrated in the particulars of collar piping, etc. The SS female auxiliaries, who carried out the same administrative and communications duties as their counterparts in other services, were trained at the Reichsschule at Oberenheim in Alsace, and instructional staff wore the cuff title in black and silver. The black and silver oval SS-runes patch with a silver edging seems to have been worn by all personnel; 'trade' patches were worn in silver/grey on black diamonds, on the forearm, as the SS eagle was always worn on the upper left sleeve. This Helferin wears

the Nazi Party button below the runes patch, and below this a bronze Reichs Sports Badge. Beige stockings and black shoes.

*G2: Germany: Führerin, Stabshelferinnen des Heeres*
The cap, jacket and skirt are in one of the many shades of field grey used by the Wehrmacht. The unusual cut of the jacket is shown here, with vertical pocket openings on the ribs, cuff tabs, and the eagle insignia worn actually on the pocket flap. For this grade the cap was piped in yellow and black along the crown seam and in the front 'scoop' of the army-shaped *Feldmütze*. The eagle, in silver on dark green, was worn on cap and breast; and for this rank the 'blitz' was in silver, with a silver cord edge to the patch. The same emblem is repeated on the black and silver enamel tie brooch. Stabshelferinnen were distinguished from Nachrichtenhelferinnen by the grey and green cuff title shown here, bearing the Gothic inscription *'Stabshelferinnen des Heeres'*. Dark grey stockings and black shoes were worn.

*G3: Italy: Auxiliary, MVSN 'Aldo Resega' Brigade*
This female auxiliary of the Fascist 'Blackshirt' organization, the MVSN, wears an all-black uniform. The large beret bears a gold fasces badge, repeated on the turned-down, rounded points of the blouse collar. The pocket flaps are straight here—for officers they were three-pointed. Wool socks and heavy mountain boots are worn

Anti-aircraft spotters on a Moscow rooftop, 1943, wearing 1940 steel helmets, stand-collar shirt-tunics in khaki, and dark blue skirts. (Novosti)

over the black stockings; there is a central front pleat in the skirt.

*H1: Soviet Union: Army nurse, 1941–43*
This nurse with the Red Army's front line troops wears a uniform indistinguishable from that of her male comrades. The khaki *pilotka* cap has the usual red and gold enamel star, hammer and sickle badge. The shirt-tunic is of the pre-1943 pattern, with falling collar, fly front and patch breast pockets. The semi-breeches, knee-boots, and rolled grey greatcoat are all standard issue; skirts were sometimes worn, but the trousers were more practical in the field. A simple sack-type kit bag holds medical supplies, slung on a cloth strap.

*H2: Soviet Union: Junior Lieutenant, Guards unit, Soviet Air Force, 1942*
The women combat aircrew of the Red Air Force wore the same insignia as their male comrades, on uniforms identical except for fitting, and the use of a khaki skirt with service dress. This young woman pilot serving with an élite Guards unit, such as the mixed-sex 73rd Guards Fighter Air Regiment, is identified as an officer by the piping in branch-of-service colour—here, air force light blue—on the collar and cuffs of her shirt-tunic. The collar patches are also in light blue, bearing the single red and gold square of junior lieutenant's rank and the winged propeller badge of the air force. A gold piping edges three sides of these officers' pattern collar patches. The exact rank is again indicated by the red and gold cloth chevrons worn on each forearm. The red, gold and white enamel badge of a Guards unit is pinned above the right breast pocket.

*H3: Yugoslavia: Partisan, 1944*
The women who travelled and fought with Tito's partisans carried out an approximation of the same duties as those of more conventional armies; caring for the sick, administering the gathering and issue of stores, and so forth. But the conditions of guerilla warfare in the harsh Balkan mountains made no more distinction between a man and a woman than did the SS and Ustachi troops who hunted the partisans. Thousands of women died in the course of the campaigns; and many fought

weapon in hand alongside their male comrades. This figure must represent the women underground fighters of all nations.

This girl wears the stone-grey Yugoslav forage cap with the red star badge of the partisans cut from cloth and sewn in place. Her motley outfit is typical: the guerillas of all nations wore what they could lay hands on. Her jacket is a captured Italian tunic with its former owner's insignia cut from sleeves and collar. The belt is courtesy of the

**Group of Red Air Force women bomber aircrew being briefed; the briefing officer seems to wear the dark blue service uniform of the Air Force, while the girls at left wear only the dark blue *pilotka*, piped light blue, with light khaki *rubaha* and semi-breeches. (Novosti)**

Waffen-SS Vth Mountain Corps, and she wears a German army waterproof shelter-half or Zeltbahn draped over her shoulders. By 1944 British supplies were reaching the partisans in some numbers, and she carries an air-dropped Sten gun; the holstered automatic is from a photograph, but unidentified.

---

## Notes sur les planches en couleur

**A1** Couvre-casquette rouge porté par tous les membres de la Police Militaire Britannique pendant le service. L'écusson de la casquette porte les lettres 'ATS' entourées d'une couronne tressée, les épaulettes ne portent que les lettres 'ATS'. La fourragère, le titre sur l'épaule 'ATS Provost' et le brassard portant les lettres 'MP' sont bleu foncé et rouges. **A2** Même uniforme de base avec le calot ATS bleu foncé et rouge avec sur la poitrine à gauche l'écusson du corps d'armée auquel elle appartient, ici l'artillerie. **A3** L'écusson en bronze du Motor Transport Corps britannique se porte sur la casquette ATS de service et est repris en plus petit sur le col. L'écusson national polonais est épinglé sur la poche gauche et on remarque une bourse en cuir marron portée sur la ceinture à droite.

**B1** Casque en acier, chemise de combat, pantalons droits et la célèbre veste militaire britannique en cuir appelée 'Trench Jerkin' sont portés pendant le service aux postes d'artillerie anti-aérienne. Les mitaines sans doigts en peau de mouton rembourrées sur le dessus proviennent de photographies. Sur l'épaule l'insigne de Anti-Aircraft Command. **B2** La casquette de service des officiers a une visière recouverte de drap; le 'A' d'Auxiliaire se porte au col et est en laiton et le rang est indiqué par un galon bleu clair sur fond bleu foncé

## Farbtafeln

**A1** Roter Mützenüberzug, von allen britischen Militärpolizisten beim Dienst getragen. Mützenemblem besteht aus den Buchstaben 'ATS' mitten in einem Kranz mit Krone obendrauf, auf den Achselklappen nur die Buchstaben 'ATS'. Achselschnur, die Bezeichnung der Einheit auf Schulterstreifen mit den Wörten 'ATS Provost' und Armbinde mit den Buchstaben 'MP' sind alle in dunkel-blau/roter Ausführung. **A2** Dieselbe Grunduniform mit der dunkel-blau/roten ATS-Feldmütze, und nur auf der linken Brust das Emblem der Waffengattung—in diesem Falle die Artillerie—an die die Frau angegliedert ist. **A3** Auf der ATS-Dienstmütze wird das bronzene Emblem des britischen Motor Transport Corps getragen, das in kleinerem Form am Kragen wiederholt wird. Auf der linken Tasche wird das polnische Nationalemblem festgesteckt und rechts am Gürtel ist ein brauner Lederbeutel gerade sichtbar.

**B1** Stahlhelm, Dienstbluse des 'Battledress', gerade geschnittene Hosen und die wohlbekannte lederne Windjacke des britischen Soldats werden bei Dienst am Flakgeschützstellung getragen. Der fingerlose Schaffellhandschuh mit aussenwärtigem Polster ist nach Photos abgezeichnet worden. Am Oberärmel wird das Abzeichen vom Anti-Aircraft Command getragen. **B2** Bei Offizieren ist der Schirm der Dienstmütze mit Tuch überzogen; ein 'A' aus Messing (d.h.

aux poignets. **B3** Les simples recrues et les sous-officiers portaient une casquette à visière de cuir noir dont l'écusson était une couronne tressée en laiton au chiffre de WAAF. L'insigne sur l'épaule représentant un albatros et le grade de toutes les simples recrues et de tous les officiers de la RAF sont en fil bleu clair sur fond bleu foncé; les simples recrues et les sous-officiers portent le 'A' sur le bras. Sacoche de masque à gaz en toile à sangles de l'armée et casque en acier peint en bleu.

**C1** Veste droite; culotte de motocycliste; entre-jambes renforcé kaki et jambières en cuir noir; casquette à visière avec lunttes protectrices en cellophane. **C2** Couvre-chef bleu foncé avec bande noire et bords relevés portant l'insigne d'officier de la RN. Remarquer les poches sans revers de la veste contrairement à celles de la simple recrue C3. Rang indiqué par un galon bleu clair. **C3** Le béret estival à dessus blanc ressemble ici beaucoup à celui des marins. Le ruban noir se termine par un noeud côté gauche et porte l'inscription HMS *Mercury* en lettres dorées, base de communications et cette femme porte sur la manche, l'écusson aux drapeaux croisés, insigne de la profession.

**D1** Cette robe et ce chapeau blancs simples étaient l'uniforme tropical le plus commun avec grade aux épaulettes, bas et chaussures blancs. **D2** Calot et robe gris ardoise avec quatre boutons bleu foncé et ceinture en tissue à deux boutons. Insigne du rang sur le calot et sur le col à gauche; ancre dorée et feuille de chêne du Navy Nurse Corps à droite. **D3** Béret haut et plat avec lanière dorée en haut sur la bande noire plutôt que sous le menton et insigne du Nurse Corps. Galon large et galon mince aux épaulettes, barrette d'officier et insigne du corps d'armée sur le col de chemise.

**E1** Le couvre-chef, la robe et la veste sans col portée au-dessus sont en tissu gris pâle 'seersucker'. L'écusson du corps d'armée WAVES, une ancre bleu clair sur hélice bleu foncé, est brodé sur les deux revers de veste. Les galons et l'insigne de la profession, plumes d'oie croisées, sont portés sur la manche gauche en bleu foncé. **E2** Le calot et le fameux blouson en laine de 1944 appelé 'Ike Jacket' sont portés par cette femme officier avec une jupe, une chemise et une cravate couleur fauve pâle. Cette veste a été avec de nombreuses variantes et peu d'officiers la porteront avec les galons aux poignets illustrés ici en liséré d'une couleur fauve plus pâle. Le passepoil doré et noir du calot indique le rang d'officier avec barrettes d'officier à gauche. Ecusson du corps d'armée à l'effigie d'Athéna sur les revers inférieurs du blouson, épaulettes du Supreme Headquarters Allied Expeditionary Force; les bandes sur la manche indiquent des périodes de six mois de service à l'étranger. **E3** Robe blanche en 'seersucker' avec boutons verts, épaulettes vertes et barrette d'officier, écussons de col USMC en bronze, casquette verte avec écusson USMC et cordon blanc.

**F1** Galons aux poignets selon le style de juin 1940 à juillet 1941; pas de passepoil au col avant octobre 1943; aigle en écusson du Luftwaffe sur la poitrine à partir de novembre 1940. Sur la poitrine écusson de radio qualifié. **F2** Garde civil de défense anti-aérienne; remarquer la coupe différente de la veste l'écusson de cet organisme sur la manche droite. Casquette de 1943 avec en écusson l'aigle de la Luftwaffe mais pas de cocarde. Chevrons sur le bras gauche. Ruban noir à la boutonnière indiquant un parent récemment tué. **F3** Calot style Luftwaffe avec passepoil brun cuivré et aigle de la Luftwaffe mais pas de cocarde. Sur la manche insigne de radio au-dessus des chevrons dans le style d'après juillet 1941. Jupe identique à F1.

**G1** Remarquer le calot inhabituel sans turban. Insigne style SS avec aigle sur le calot et la manche gauche, chiffre SS sur l'insigne de poitrine. Insigne de radiophoniste style SS sur l'avant-bras gauche au-dessus de la lisière de poignet portant l'inscription 'Reichsschule'. Ecusson sportif et bouton de membre du parti sur la poitrine à gauche sous le chiffre SS. **G2** Calot de l'armée, cordon en passepoil jaune/noir posé en couronne et sur le devant du turban insigne de l'armée représentant l'aigle. Remarquer la coupe inhabituelle de la veste. Insigne de radiophoniste représentant un éclair sur la manche et broche de cravate; lisière de poignet avec l'inscription 'Stabshelferinnen des Heeres' en vert sur gris. **G3** Uniforme entièrement noir consistant d'un béret, d'une chemise, veste, jupe, bas et chaussures de marche avec sur le béret l'insigne doré représentant l'aigle fasciste ainsi que sur le col de chemise. Les officiers avaient des pattes de poche pointues.

**H1** Uniforme simple identique à celui du reste de l'Armée Rouge dans le style d'avant 1943. Le seul insigne est l'étoile rouge sur le calot appelé *Pilotka*. Grand manteau kaftan enroulé avec une simple sacoche de fournitures médicales portée également en bandoulière. **H2** Passepoil bleu au col et poignets identifiant un officier d'aviation, chevrons rouges et dorés sur la manche, bouton doré et rouge sur les empiècements de col indiquant le grade exact; empiècements de col bleus portant des hélices à ailes dorées identifiant l'aviation. Insigne du régiment des gardes sur la poitrine. **H3** Silhouette représentative symbolisant toutes les femmes qui se battiront au sein des troupes de partisans dans toute l'Europe occupée. Cette femme-ci porte le calot yougoslave avec l'étoile rouge, une vieille tunique italienne, une ceinture allemande et un poncho camouflé, des pantalons civils et enfin un fusil mitrailleur britannique Sten.

'Auxiliary'—Hilfstruppen) wird am Kragen getragen und auf jedem Ärmel besteht das Rangabzeichen aus einem hellblauem Streifen auf dunklerer blauer Grundfarbe. **B3** Bei Unteroffizieren und Mannschaften war der Mützenschirm in schwarzem Leder ausgeführt, das Messingemblem an der Mütze bestand aus dem WAAF-Monogramm im Kranz mit Krone obendrauf. Das von sämtlichen Unteroffizieren und Mannschaften des RAF getragen Albatrosschulteremblem und Dienstgradabzeichen mit hellblauem Faden auf dunkelblauer Unterlage gestickt, alle Unteroffiziere und Mannschaft trugen dazu da 'A'. Militär Gasmaskenbeutel aus Gurtzeug, blau bemahlener Stahlhelm.

**C1** Einreihige Jacke; Motorradhose mit Khakiverstärkung zwischen den Beinen und hohe Gamaschen aus schwarzem Leder; Schirmmütze mit Zellophanschützbrille. **C2** Dunkelblauer Hut mit schwarzem Band und Krempenumrandung und Mützenabzeichen des RN-Offiziers. Bemerkenswert ist die Tasche ohne Patte, im Gegensatz zu der in C3 abgebildeten Uniform der Unteroffiziere und Mannschaft. **C3** Die Mütze, hier mit weissem Sommerbezug geschildert, war der Matrosenmütze sehr ähnlich. Der schwarze Band war auf der linken Seite mit einer Schleife befestigt und trug den Schiffsnamen in Goldbuchstaben—HMS *Mercury* war ein Nachrichtensammelstützpunkt, und dieses Mädchen trägt auf ihrem Ärmel die geschränkten Fahnen als Abzeichen des Dienstgewerbes.

**D1** Dieses ganz einfache weisse Kleid mit Hut waren normale Tropenkleidung, mit Rangabzeichen auf den Achselklappen; weisse Strümpfe und Schuhe. **D2** Mütze und Kleid aus 'schiefergrauem' Stoffe mit vier dunkelblauen Knöpfen und einen Stoffgürtel mit doppelter Knopfbefestigung. Rechts auf der Mütze und am Kragen befinden sich Rangabzeichen und auf der linken Seite das goldene Anker und Eichenblattemblem des Navy Nurse Corps. **D3** Schirmlose Mütze mit hohem Vorderteil und mit goldenem Sturmemblem oben anstatt unten am schwarzen Hutband, sowohl als Emblem des Nurse Corps. Die Streifen—ein breiter und ein dünner—die den Rang bezeichnen befinden sich auf den Achselklappen und auf dem Hemdkragen Rangstreifen und Korpsinsignien.

**E1** Mütze, Kleid und obendrauf getragene kragenlose Jacke sind alle aus hellgrauem 'seersucker' Stoffe hergestellt. Das Gattungsabzeichen der WAVES—ein leuchtend blauer Anker auf dunkelblauer Schiffsschraube wird gestickt auf beiden Aufschlägen der Jacke getragen. Dienstgradabzeichen und die geschränkten Federkiele des Dienstgewerbes werden in dunkelblau auf dem linken Ärmel getragen. **E2** Die 'Überseemütze' und wollene 'Ike Jacket' 1944 Musters werden zusammen mit hellbeigem Rock, Hemd und Schlips von diesem Offizier getragen. Die Jackeneinzelheiten waren in vielen Beziehungen unterschiedlich; nur wenige davon waren mit der hier geschilderten aus heller beiger Tresse hergestellten Offiziersärmelaufschlagstreifen ausgestattet. Offizierstand wird durch den gold/schwarzen Mützenschnurbesatz bezeichnet; auf der linken Seite befinden sich die Rangstreifen. Auf den unteren Jackenaufschlägen sieht man das Korpsemblem, den Athenakopf; Schulterabzeichen des Oberkommandos der alliierten Expeditionskorps; die am Ärmel angebrachten Streifen bezeichnen je sechs Monate Überseedienst. **E3** Weisses 'seersucker'—Kleid mit grünen Knöpfen, grüne Achselklappen mit goldenen Rangstreifen, bronze USMC-Kragenabzeichen; grüne Mütze mit USMC-Emblem und weissen Schnüren.

**F1** Rangsabzeichen auf den Ärmelaufschlägen, wie zwischen Juni 1940– Juli 1941 getragen; Kragen war bis Oktober 1943 ohne Schnurbesatz; Luftwaffe November 1940 Adleremblem auf der Brust. Ärmel abzeichen eines geprüften Funkunteroffiziers. **F2** Zivil Luftschutzwart; bemerkenswert ist der Unterschied am Schnitt der Jacke. 1943 Einheitsfeldmütze mit Luftwaffenadleremblem, jedoch ohne Kokarde. Dienstgradwinkel am linken Arm. Der schwarze Band am Knopfloch bezeichnet, dass ein Verwandter neulich gefallen ist. **F3** Luftwaffenartige Feldmütze mit kupferbraunem Schnurbesatz und Luftwaffenadler, aber ohne Kokarde. Funkerärmelabzeichen der Dienstgradwinkel nach-Juli 1941 Musters. Rock wie bei F1.

**G1** Bemerkenswert ist die aussergewöhnliche aufschlaglose Einheitsfeldmütze. SS-artige Embleme auf Mütze und linkem Ärmel, SS-Runen auf dem Brustemblem. Am linken Unterarm Funkerabzeichen SS-Musters oberhalb des Ärmelaufschlagbandes worauf 'Reichsschule' steht. An der linken Brust unterhalb der SS-Runen befinden sich Sport- und Parteimitgliedembleme. **G2** Feldmütze des Heerenmusters mit gelb/schwarzem Schnurbesatz am Scheitel und am vorderen Aufschlag und Heeresadleremblem. Bemerkenswert ist der aussergewöhnliche Schnitt der Jacke. Funkerblitzabzeichen am Ärmel und Schlipsbroche; Ärmelaufschlagband worauf 'Stabshelferinnen des Heeres' grün auf grauem Grunde steht. **G3** Durchaus schwarze Uniform besteht aus Baskenmütze, Bluse, Jacke, Rock, Strümpfen und starken Schuhen mit goldenem Faschistenemblem auf der Baskenmütze und dem Blusenkragen. Offiziere trugen spitze Taschenpatten.

**H1** Einfache Uniform, mit dem Rest der Rotarmee identisch, vor-1943 Musters; als einziges Abzeichen der rote Stern am *pilotka* Feldmütze. Der graue *kaftan* Wintermantel wird aufgerollt um den Körper gehängt; einfacher Beutel mit Arzneimittel wird auch auf einem Riemen umgehängt. **H2** Durch blauem Schurbesatz am Kragen und an den Armelaufschlägen wird diese als Offizier der Fliegerabteilung erkannt; Ärmelwinkel in rot und gold und rot/goldene Knöpfe auf den Tuchabzeichen am Kragen bezeichnen den genauen Dienstgrad; die Fliegerabteilung wird durch die blauen Tuchabzeichen am Kragen mit goldener geflügelter Luftschraube gekennzeichnet. An der Brust das Emblem des Gardergiments. **H3** Eine symbolische Figur, die alle Frauen symbolisiert, die durch die ganzen Besatzungsgebiete Europas mit den Partisanbanden gekämpft haben. Sie trägt die jugoslawische Feldmütze mit rotem Sternemblem, einen alten italienischen Waffenrock, deutschen Gürtel und Zeltbahn, Zivilhosen und sie hält in der Hand eine britische Sten-maschinenpistole.